T0291272

JOB SATISFACTION

Distilling the vast literature on this most frequently studied variable in organizational behavior, Paul E. Spector provides students and professionals with a pithy overview of the research and application of job satisfaction.

In addition to discussing the nature of and techniques for assessing job satisfaction, this text summarizes the findings regarding how people feel toward work, including cultural and gender differences in job satisfaction, personal and organizational antecedents, potential consequences, and interventions to improve job satisfaction. Students, researchers, and practitioners will particularly appreciate the extensive list of references and the Job Satisfaction Survey included in the Appendix. This book includes the latest research and new topics including the business case for job satisfaction, customer service, disabled workers, leadership, mental health, organizational climate, virtual work, and work-family issues. Further, paulspector.com features an ongoing series of blog articles, links to assessments mentioned in the book, and other resources on job satisfaction to coincide with this text.

This book is ideal for professionals, researchers, and undergraduate and graduate students in industrial and organizational psychology and organizational behavior, as well as in specialized courses on job attitudes or job satisfaction.

Paul E. Spector is Distinguished Professor Emeritus at the University of South Florida, USA. He currently teaches Executive Doctor of Business Administration students in the Muma College of Business at the University of South Florida.

JOB SATISFACTION

From Assessment to Intervention

Paul E. Spector

Routledge
Taylor & Francis Group

NEW YORK AND LONDON

Cover image: fizkes / Getty Images

First published 2022
by Routledge
605 Third Avenue, New York, NY 10158

and by Routledge
4 Park Square, Milton Park, Abingdon, Oxon, OX14 4RN

Routledge is an imprint of the Taylor & Francis Group, an informa business

Library of Congress Cataloging-in-Publication Data
Names: Spector, Paul E., author.
Title: Job satisfaction : from assessment to intervention / Paul E. Spector.
Description: Abingdon, Oxon ; New York, NY : Routledge, 2022. | "This book updates my Job Satisfaction: Application, Assessment, Causes, and Consequences published in 1997"—Preface. | Includes bibliographical references and index.
Identifiers: LCCN 2021041891 (print) | LCCN 2021041892 (ebook) | ISBN 9781032168524 (hardback) | ISBN 9781032168500 (paperback) | ISBN 9781003250616 (ebook)
Subjects: LCSH: Job satisfaction.
Classification: LCC HF5549.5.J63 S636 2022 (print) | LCC HF5549.5.J63 (ebook) | DDC 158.7—dc23
LC record available at https://lccn.loc.gov/2021041891
LC ebook record available at https://lccn.loc.gov/2021041892

ISBN: 9781032168524 (hbk)
ISBN: 9781032168500 (pbk)
ISBN: 9781003250616 (ebk)

DOI: 10.4324/9781003250616

Typeset in Joanna
by codeMantra

CONTENTS

FIGURES

TABLES

PREFACE

Job satisfaction is the degree to which people like their jobs. Some people enjoy work and find it to be a central part of their lives. Others hate their jobs and go to work only because they must. The study of how people feel about their jobs—whether they like or hate working—is one of the major topics in the fields of business management and industrial-organizational psychology. More studies have been done to understand job satisfaction than any other variable in organizational research on people. In addition, the assessment of employee attitudes such as job satisfaction has become a common activity in organizations where management is concerned with the physical and psychological well-being of employees.

This book will provide an overview of the vast job satisfaction research literature. Although the primary focus is on the findings and theories from the academic literature, we will also pay some attention to applications conducted within organizations to improve efficiency and quality of working life. Job satisfaction is associated with many important behaviors and outcomes for employees that have implications for organizational and personal well-being.

This book is intended to be an introduction to the topic of job satisfaction. By necessity it provides only an overview of the major issues and research findings, as a detailed treatment of this topic would require several volumes. Some familiarity with basic research methodology would be helpful. Although the book is not particularly technical, there are a few statistical terms used, such as the correlation coefficient.

This book is organized into eight chapters. Chapter 1 discusses the nature of job satisfaction, including what it is and why it is an important topic for concern in organizations. The chapter will make the business case that job satisfaction is important. The assessment of job satisfaction is the topic of Chapter 2. Both the development of new scales and the use of existing scales are covered, as well as issues when job satisfaction scales are translated and used in a new language. Chapter 3 focuses on how people feel about work. Included will be findings on job satisfaction differences for various demographic groups, as well as cross-country comparisons. Environmental factors that might affect job satisfaction are covered in Chapter 4, including characteristics of jobs, job stress, leadership, and how employees are treated. Chapter 5 is concerned with individual difference in job satisfaction that might result in different employees feeling differently about the same job. The fit between person and job is also covered. Chapter 6 focuses on the behavior of employees that might be the result or the cause of job satisfaction. Chapter 7 looks at the health and well-being of employees and how it is linked to job satisfaction. The final chapter is concerned with interventions that can be used to improve job satisfaction.

This book updates my *Job Satisfaction: Application, Assessment, Causes, and Consequences* published in 1997. We have learned a great deal in the 25 years since that book was published. Many new topics have been added throughout, including:

- The business case for job satisfaction
- Customer service
- Descent work
- Disabled workers
- Job attitudes of organizational commitment, occupational commitment, job involvement, and engagement
- Justice
- Leadership
- Mental health
- Neurodiversity
- Organizational climate

- Organizational performance
- Translating job satisfaction instruments
- Virtual work

A new chapter on interventions has been added. A new appendix has links to resources on my website that include all the job satisfaction instruments discussed in the book, an assessment archive with instruments used in job satisfaction research, a blog on topics related to job satisfaction, and other features concerning job satisfaction.

No one writes a book such as this one without the assistance of others. I would like to thank the anonymous reviewers who provided helpful advice on the original plan that helped shape the final product. I would also like to thank my Routledge editor, Christina Chronister, as well as the following people at Routledge who helped at various stages along the way including my Production Editor Kelly Cracknell, Editorial Assistant Priya Sharma, Project Manager Nazrine Azeez, and Copy Editor Jijendrakumar P.

Paul E. Spector

1

THE NATURE OF JOB
SATISFACTION

Every year the U.S. Federal government surveys its employees to find out among other things how employees feel about their jobs. Since 2004, the U.S. Congress has required as part of the National Defense Authorization Act that employees be assessed on both the leadership practices that affect agency performance and on their job satisfaction (U.S. Office of Personnel Management, 2008). This includes satisfaction with leadership, the work environment, rewards, and personal growth. Clearly the U.S. Congress recognizes the central importance of employee job satisfaction for the effective operation of its agencies.

Job satisfaction is a topic of wide interest, not only to the U.S. Federal government but to both people who work in organizations (employees and leaders) and people who study them. In fact, it is the most frequently studied variable in academic research on people at work. It is a central variable in both research and theory of organizational phenomena ranging from job design to supervision. Literally thousands of job satisfaction studies can be found in the journals of industrial-organizational psychology,

DOI: 10.4324/9781003250616-1

organizational behavior, and many other fields such as counseling, criminology, education, and nursing, just to name a few.

What Is Job Satisfaction?

Job satisfaction is simply how people feel about their jobs and different aspects of their jobs. It is the extent to which people like (satisfaction) or dislike (dissatisfaction) their jobs. As it is generally assessed, job satisfaction is an attitude. That means it reflects people's evaluations of the job along a continuum from favorable to unfavorable. As Weiss (2002) explains, often job satisfaction is described as an emotional reaction to the job, but satisfaction is better considered as more of a cognitive reaction—a weighing of whether a job is good or bad from a personal perspective. As we will see later in the book, job satisfaction is related to emotional responses to work, but it is not the same thing.

In the past, job satisfaction was approached by some researchers from the perspective of need fulfillment, that is, whether or not the job meets the employee's physical and psychological needs for the things provided by work such as pay or making social connections with others (e.g., Wolf, 1970). However, this approach has been abandoned as today most researchers focus attention on job satisfaction as an attitude.

Job satisfaction can be considered as a global evaluation of the job or as a related constellation of attitudes about various aspects or facets of the job. The global approach is used when the overall or bottom-line attitude is of interest, for example, if one wishes to determine the effects of people liking or disliking their jobs. Most of the research I will discuss assessed global job satisfaction in relation to other variables of interest. The facet approach is used to find out how satisfied people are with different aspects of the job, such as coworkers or pay. This can be very useful for organizations that wish to identify areas of dissatisfaction that they can improve. Sometimes both approaches can be used to get a complete picture of employee job satisfaction.

A job satisfaction facet can be concerned with any aspect or part of a job. Facets frequently assessed include rewards such as pay or fringe benefits, other people such as coworkers or supervisors, the nature of the work itself, and the organization. Table 1.1 contains facets that can be found in some of the most popular job satisfaction instruments, which will be

Table 1.1 Common Job Satisfaction Facets

Facet	Description
Appreciation	People value what you do.
Communication	How well management communicates.
Coworkers	Peers you work with.
Fringe benefits	Insurance, vacation time, and other benefits.
Job conditions	The environment in which you work.
Nature of the work itself	The tasks that you do.
Organization itself	Overall feelings about the employer.
Organization's policies	How the organization operates.
Pay	Salary and other financial rewards.
Personal growth	Learning new knowledge and skill.
Promotion opportunities	Ability to move into a higher position.
Recognition	Getting praise for good work.
Security	Little chance of being laid off.
Supervision	The person you report to.

discussed in the next chapter of this book. Sometimes organizations will be interested in very specific facets not found in an existing scale, such as satisfaction with policies or practices unique to that organization.

The facet approach can provide a more complete picture of a person's job satisfaction than the global approach. An employee can have very different feelings about the various facets. He or she might like coworkers and dislike pay, a common pattern for North Americans. As we will see in Chapter 3, however, patterns can be different in other countries or regions of the world.

Not only do people differ in their satisfaction across facets, but the facets are only modestly related to one another. Table 1.2 contains inter-correlations among the nine facets of the Job Satisfaction Survey or JSS (Spector, 1985), which is one of the satisfaction instruments discussed in Chapter 2. As can be seen, the correlations among many of the facets tend to be rather small, for example, the correlation between satisfaction with pay and supervision is 0.19. This pattern of results is convincing evidence that people have distinctly different attitudes about the various facets of the job. They tend not to have an overall feeling that produces the same level of satisfaction with every job facet.

There has been a lot of work conducted to determine the underlying structure of job satisfaction facets, that is, what are the major aspects that people distinguish when they think about their jobs. Most studies have used complex statistics (e.g., factor analysis) to reduce people's responses to

Table 1.2 Intercorrelations among JSS Subscales

Facet	1	2	3	4	5	6	7	8
1. Pay								
2. Promotion	0.53							
3. Supervision	0.19	0.25						
4. Benefits	0.45	0.36	0.10					
5. Contingent rewards	0.54	0.58	0.46	0.38				
6. Operating procedures	0.31	0.31	0.17	0.29	0.46			
7. Coworkers	0.19	0.23	0.42	0.16	0.39	0.22		
8. Nature of work	0.25	0.32	0.31	0.20	0.47	0.30	0.32	
9. Communication	0.40	0.45	0.39	0.30	0.59	0.44	0.42	0.43

From Spector (1985).

Note: n = 3,027. All correlations are significant at $p < 0.001$.

many satisfaction items to a small number of underlying dimensions of job satisfaction. These studies, summarized by Locke (1976), have suggested several structures. They clearly separate facets into four areas:

- Nature of Work: The tasks done on the job.
- Organizational Context: Policies and practices.
- Rewards: Benefits and pay.
- Social Environment: Coworkers and supervisors.

The intercorrelations among the facets in Table 1.2 are consistent with this structure in that a facet correlates more strongly with other facets in its own area than facets in other areas. For example, the reward facets of fringe benefits and pay correlate more strongly with one another than with the organizational context facets of communication or operating procedures.

The Business Case for Job Satisfaction

There are important reasons that we should be concerned with job satisfaction, which can be classified according to the focus on the employee or organization. First, the humanitarian perspective is that people deserve to be treated fairly and with respect. Because work is such an important part of people's lives, what happens at work can have a huge impact on both physical and mental well-being. Job satisfaction is to some extent a reflection of good treatment by the employer. It can be considered an over-all indicator of work adjustment. Having employees with low job satisfaction suggests problems in how employees are being managed and treated. A broad stakeholder perspective says that organizations have a responsibility to all people who are affected by them including employees. Making efforts to enhance job satisfaction is the right thing to do from an ethical and moral perspective.

Second, the utilitarian perspective is that job satisfaction can lead to behavior by employees that affects organizational functioning. This is the perspective than many would consider the "business case", that is, how does employee job satisfaction affect organizational functioning and the bottom line. As you will see later in this book, there are important implications of employee job satisfaction that has the potential to affect both positive (e.g., customer service) and negative (e.g., turnover) behaviors. It has been linked not only to important employee outcomes, but to organizational performance as well. Furthermore, job satisfaction can reflect how well an organization is managed and is functioning. It can indicate problems in leadership or in the organization of work. Differences among organizational units in job satisfaction can be diagnostic of potential trouble-spots. Each reason is sufficient to justify concern with job satisfaction. Combined they explain and justify the attention that is paid to this important variable.

Managers in many organizations, such as U.S. Federal government, share the concerns of researchers for the job satisfaction of employees. The assessment of job satisfaction is a common activity in these organizations where management feels that employee well-being is important, and actions are taken to correct potential problems that surveys uncover. In the rest of this book, I will discuss factors that might influence job satisfaction, and ramifications of this variable for employees and organizations. At the end, I will discuss some of the interventions that organizations use to enhance job satisfaction of their employees.

Related Job Attitudes

Job satisfaction is the most studied and measured job attitude, but it is not the only one. There are many attitude variables that are conceptually distinct from job satisfaction and from one another. They are all related to job satisfaction and can relate similarly to the same things.

Organizational Commitment

Organizational commitment is the attachment that an individual has for their current employer rather than how much the individual likes or dislikes the job. Mowday (1998) notes that commitment has three interrelated components that form a single global concept:

- Accepting the organization's goals and values.
- Willingness to work hard for the organization.
- Desire to stay with the organization.

Note that the focus of this attitude is solely on the organization itself, whereas job satisfaction is focused more on the job and facets of the job.

Meyer, Allen, and Smith (1993) developed the idea that there are three distinct types of commitment.

- Affective commitment is the attitudinal component that most closely aligns with the original unidimensional conception of Mowday, Steers, and Porter (1979). It is aligned with a person's emotional attachment to the job and reflects how much a person wants to remain with the employer.
- Continuance commitment is based on what would be lost (e.g., pension benefits) by leaving the organization. A person might want to keep a job that is dissatisfying because of the need to keep benefits or the inability to find another job that pays as well, often referred to as golden handcuffs as a generous salary and benefit package can trap a person in a particular job.
- Normative commitment is based on values and the extent to which a person feels an obligation to stay. An individual might remain on a dissatisfying job out of loyalty to an organization or supervisor. For example, if an organization funds an employee's education, that could create a sense of obligation.

Like job satisfaction, organizational commitment is normally assessed with employee self-report surveys, the most popular being the global organizational commitment scale that produces a single score reflecting primarily affective commitment (Mowday et al., 1979), or the three-component organizational commitment scale (Allen & Meyer, 1996). Studies that have assessed it along with job satisfaction have found that affective commitment (whether measured with the Mowday et al. or Allen and Meyer scale) is related to global job satisfaction, and among satisfaction facets is most strongly related to work itself and is least strongly related to pay.

Occupational Commitment

Whereas organizational commitment concerns the bond of employees with their employers, occupational commitment is the attachment a person has to an occupation. This means the person has a strong desire to remain in the occupation, although is not necessarily committed to the current employer. People vary in their occupational commitment, and it is not unusual to see someone, even after spending years pursing an advanced professional degree, to switch occupations. Thus, we might see an attorney give up law career or a certified public accountant give up an accounting career.

Occupational commitment is considered an attitude much like affective organizational commitment (Lee, Carswell, & Allen, 2000). In their meta-analysis (a study that quantitatively combines results of prior studies), Lee et al. (2000) found that it related to other job attitudes, including job satisfaction, affective commitment, and job involvement (discussed next). As with affective commitment, it was most strongly related to the job satisfaction facet of work itself and least strongly related to the facet of pay.

Job Involvement

Job involvement is the importance of work for an individual, that is, the extent to which their job is a major part of their sense of self-worth (Lodahl & Kejnar, 1965). A person who is high on job involvement prioritizes their job over other activities. Job involvement is distinct from other job attitudes, as its focus is on the value of work itself and not a particular employer, job, or occupation. This suggests that a person might have high job involvement, even though their commitment or satisfaction is low for their current employer and job.

As with occupational commitment, job involvement relates to both global job satisfaction and organizational commitment (see meta-analysis by Brown, 1996). It correlates most strongly with the facet of work satisfaction, and least strongly with the facet of pay satisfaction, a pattern you have already seen with other job attitudes. This is not surprising because job involvement focuses on work itself as opposed to other aspects of a job.

Employee Engagement

Employee engagement is a relatively new construct that has captured the attention of managers and practitioners. Many organizations have transitioned from periodically assessing job satisfaction of their employees to measuring engagement. As it is typically measured by consultants and practitioners, engagement is more encompassing than job satisfaction, as it assesses elements of attitudes, behavior, and personality. Measures often include elements of commitment, emotion, and effort (Macey & Schneider, 2008). Such scales that include items reflecting a variety of constructs can be problematic because two people might have the same score for different reasons; one employee might be highly committed but make little effort while another employee has the opposite pattern. Further, total scores do not shed much light on the specific areas of concern.

Schaufeli, Salanova, González-Romá, and Bakker (2002) developed a multidimensional conception of employee engagement that contains separate elements reflecting attitudes and motivation. According to this view, engagement is concerned with the extent to which people feel connected and expend energy toward the job. It is reflected in three dimensions:

- Vigor: How energized someone feels about work.
- Dedication: Enthusiasm for the job.
- Absorption: The extent to which employees become immersed in work and enjoy doing it.

The focus of engagement is the immediate job and the tasks that are being performed. Not surprisingly global engagement is related to job involvement, job satisfaction (Eldor & Harpaz, 2016) and organizational commitment (Saks, 2006). All three engagement dimensions are related to job satisfaction (Lu, Lu, Gursoy, & Neale, 2016) and organizational commitment (Reijseger et al., 2013).

Why Is There So Much Attention Paid to Job Satisfaction?

Job satisfaction became a topic of research in the middle 1930s in the U.S. Many attribute the beginning of job satisfaction research to the book *Job Satisfaction* by Robert Hoppock (1935). In it he describes his research and provides a measuring instrument that others used for subsequent studies. Around that time we see early publications, not only by Hoppock on age and satisfaction (Hoppock, 1936), but by prominent researchers like Arthur Kornhauser (Kornhauser & Sharp, 1932) who was one of the early researchers studying workplace health and well-being. Although Hoppock did much to launch interest in job satisfaction, the idea had been around for a while. For example, in 1917 Edward Thorndike was doing laboratory experiments on what he called the satisfyingness of work by having subjects perform a boring task for a period of time (Thorndike, 1917) and then measuring their reactions.

Interest in job satisfaction took decades to develop, but today it is the most researched topics in organizational research. I did a search on the Clarivate Analytics (Web of Science) database for the topic "job satisfaction" on June 11, 2021. There were a total of 36,653 publications on the topic spread across a wide variety of disciplines including behavioral sciences, business, education, health sciences, psychology, public health, and social sciences. Figure 1.1 shows the number of publications per decade from the first in the database in 1936 until June of 2021. As can be seen in the figure, there was an acceleration in the number of publications per decade that continues to this day. There were only 8 publications in the decade of the 1930s (1930–1939), 24 in the 1940s, 103 in the 1950s and so on. In 2020 alone there were 4,188 publications. It would take from 1936 to 1988 for the field to amass that number of publications on the topic of job satisfaction.

The assessment of job satisfaction is an activity performed by both academic researchers and practitioners alike. The goal of those who publish academic research, whether they be professors at universities, research scientists in research institutes, or practitioners is to contribute to scientific knowledge. They often include job satisfaction in their research studies to provide an expanded understanding of people's experiences at work, and job satisfaction has served a central role in many investigations. Some focus

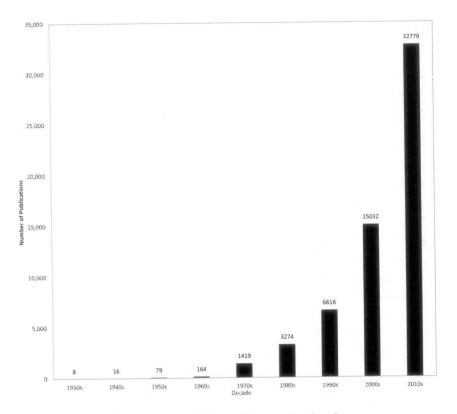

Figure 1.1 The number of job satisfaction publications by decade.

on potential antecedents or drivers of positive employee attitudes. Others focus on the potential consequences for employees, other stakeholders (e.g., customers) and organizations. Still others might look for boundary conditions, such as conditions under which job satisfaction might or might not lead to an important outcome.

For the practitioner, job satisfaction represents a metric that reflects on the human resource health of an organization. Many organizations, like the U.S. federal government benchmark satisfaction, tracking it from year to year to identify areas of needed improvement. The use of questionnaires, easily administered online in most cases, allows for quantification of job satisfaction that makes it possible to compare across subunits and time. Job satisfaction can be considered an important outcome to be managed with appropriate interventions, and it can be considered an important indicator of organizational trouble-spots needing attention.

The remaining chapters will provide an overview of how people generally feel about work, and what might serve as antecedents or drivers of job satisfaction and potential outcomes. But first I turn to how job satisfaction is assessed.

References

Allen, N. J., & Meyer, J. P. (1996). Affective, continuance, and normative commitment to the organization: An examination of construct validity. *Journal of Vocational Behavior, 49*, 252–276. doi: 10.1006/jvbe.1996.0043

Brown, S. P. (1996). A meta-analysis and review of organizational research on job involvement. *Psychological Bulletin, 120*, 235–255. doi: 10.1037/0033-2909.120.2.235

Eldor, L., & Harpaz, I. (2016). A process model of employee engagement: The learning climate and its relationship with extra-role performance behaviors. *Journal of Organizational Behavior, 37*, 213–235. doi: 10.1002/job.2037

Hoppock, R. (1935). *Job satisfaction*. New York: Harper and Brothers.

Hoppock, R. (1936). Age and job satisfaction. *Psychological Monographs, 47*, 115–118. doi: 10.1037/h0093408

Kornhauser, A., & Sharp, A. (1932). Employee attitudes; suggestions from a study in a factory. *Personnel Journal, 10*, 393–404.

Lee, K., Carswell, J. J., & Allen, N. J. (2000). A meta-analytic review of occupational commitment: Relations with person- and work-related variables. *Journal of Applied Psychology, 85*, 799–811. doi: 10.1037/0021-9010.85.5.799

Locke, E. A. (1976). The nature and causes of job satisfaction. In M. D. Dunnette (Ed.), *Handbook of industrial and organizational psychology* (pp. 1297–1349). Chicago, IL: Rand McNally.

Lodahl, T. M., & Kejnar, M. (1965). The definition and measurement of job involvement. *Journal of Applied Psychology, 49*, 24–33. doi: 10.1037/h0021692

Lu, L., Lu, A. C. C., Gursoy, D., & Neale, N. R. (2016). Work engagement, job satisfaction, and turnover intentions: A comparison between supervisors and line-level employees. *International Journal of Contemporary Hospitality Management, 28*, 737–761. doi: 10.1108/IJCHM-07-2014-0360

Macey, W. H., & Schneider, B. (2008). The meaning of employee engagement. *Industrial and Organizational Psychology, 1*, 3–30. doi: 10.1111/j.1754-9434.2007.0002.x

Meyer, J. P., Allen, N. J., & Smith, C. A. (1993). Commitment to organizations and occupations: Extension and test of a three-component conceptualization. *Journal of Applied Psychology, 78*, 538–551. doi: 10.1037/0021-9010.78.4.538

Mowday, R. T. (1998). Reflections on the study and relevance of organizational commitment. *Human Resource Management Review, 8*, 387–401. doi: 10.1016/S1053-4822(99)00006-6

Mowday, R. T., Steers, R. M., & Porter, L. W. (1979). The measurement of organizational commitment. *Journal of Vocational Behavior, 14*, 224–247.

Reijseger, G., Schaufeli, W. B., Peeters, M. C. W., Taris, T. W., van Beek, I., & Ouweneel, E. (2013). Watching the paint dry at work: Psychometric examination of the Dutch Boredom Scale. *Anxiety, Stress & Coping: An International Journal, 26*, 508–525. doi: 10.1080/10615806.2012.720676

Saks, A. M. (2006). Antecedents and consequences of employee engagement. *Journal of Managerial Psychology, 21*, 600–619. doi: 10.1108/02683940610690169

Schaufeli, W. B., Salanova, M., González-Romá, V., & Bakker, A. B. (2002). The measurement of engagement and burnout: A two sample confirmatory factor analytic approach. *Journal of Happiness Studies: An Interdisciplinary Forum on Subjective Well-Being, 3*, 71–92. doi: 10.1023/A:1015630930326

Spector, P. E. (1985). Measurement of human service staff satisfaction: Development of the Job Satisfaction Survey. *American Journal of Community Psychology, 13*, 693–713. doi: 10.1007/BF00929796

Thorndike, E. L. (1917). The curve of work and the curve of satisfyingness. *Journal of Applied Psychology, 1*, 265–267. doi: 10.1037/h0074929

U.S. Office of Personnel Management. (2008). Annual employee survey guidance, Retrieved May 17, 2021, from https://www.opm.gov/policy-data-oversight/data-analysis-documentation/employee-surveys/surveyguidance.pdf

Weiss, H. M. (2002). Deconstructing job satisfaction: Separating evaluations, beliefs and affective experiences. *Human Resource Management Review, 12*, 173–194. doi: 10.1016/S1053-4822(02)00045-1

Wolf, M. G. (1970). Need gratification theory: a theoretical reformulation of job satisfaction/dissatisfaction and job motivation. *Journal of Applied Psychology, 54*, 87–94. doi: 10.1037/h0028664

2

THE ASSESSMENT OF JOB SATISFACTION

Job satisfaction is usually measured with questionnaires administered to employees. Other approaches such as interviews are certainly possible but are less often used due to greater cost. One can survey many people with a questionnaire, especially when conducted online, with comparatively little effort or expense. Furthermore, it is easy to quantify and standardize questionnaire responses. However, it is possible to get more extensive information in an interview, as respondents can elaborate about their issues. In addition, the less constrained format of an interview allows for the emergence of points that are not preplanned by the interviewer. The interviewees can generate their own areas of satisfaction or dissatisfaction and raise their own issues.

The interview is particularly helpful as an initial step in a job satisfaction survey project whether conducted for academic research or practice. For academic research, interviews can help identify the specific variables that should be assessed, which is very helpful as a first step as you begin studying a new topic. This helps you get a basic understanding of how people

DOI: 10.4324/9781003250616-2

feel about their jobs in the context of what you wish to study. For the practitioner, interviews can uncover the specific issues that are of concern to the employees who will be subsequently surveyed with a questionnaire. This allows for a more precise assessment than just using general facets from an existing satisfaction instrument. For example, using a standard measure of fringe benefit satisfaction might suggest that employees are not very satisfied with this facet, but an interview could indicate that it is only the health insurance provided that is the source of dissatisfaction. Including a targeted question about health insurance would provide an indication of how widespread that dissatisfaction might be.

There have been a few attempts to use alternative procedures to assess job satisfaction. Spector, Dwyer, and Jex (1988) asked supervisors to estimate the job satisfaction of their subordinates. The correlation was 0.54 between incumbents and supervisors, suggesting that the supervisors may have been very aware of their subordinates' job satisfaction. Glick, Jenkins, and Gupta (1986) had observers estimate people's job satisfaction after watching them work for about two hours. Again, there was moderate agreement between the two sources. There has even been a study where elementary school children were asked to estimate the satisfaction of their parents (Trice & Tillapaugh, 1991), and a study in which husbands were asked about their wives' satisfaction with being working mothers (Barling & Macewen, 1988). In both studies there was reasonable agreement between employees and their family members. Of course, in no case is the agreement high enough to conclude that the alternative sources are equivalent to asking the individuals directly about their own job satisfaction.

The easiest way to assess job satisfaction is to use one of the existing survey instruments rather than developing one from scratch. Several have been carefully developed and are easily accessible. Some of the most popular among academic researchers are discussed in this chapter.

There are five advantages to using an existing job satisfaction instrument. First, many of the available instruments cover the major facets of satisfaction. Often these facets are those of interest in a satisfaction survey, whether conducted for academic or applied purposes. Second, most existing instruments have been used enough times to provide norms, which are the means on each facet for people within a given population, such as all private sector managers in the U.S. Comparisons of your results with norms can help with the interpretation of results.

Third, many existing instruments have been shown to exhibit acceptable levels of reliability. Reliability refers to consistency in measurement, that is, if we repeatedly assess job satisfaction of a person will we get the same number each time, assuming the person's attitudes do not change? Of most concern with instruments that contain multiple items is that those items are internally consistent, meaning they are strongly related to one another. This is reflected in the coefficient alpha statistic for which the widely accepted minimum standard is a value of at least 0.70 for academic research but ideally more than 0.80 for applied uses (Nunnally, 1978).

Fourth, their use in research provides good evidence for construct validity. Validity concerns our interpretation of what an instrument reflects, that is, does our job satisfaction instrument assess people's feelings concerning their jobs? Some instruments might not reflect what we intend to measure. If employees are concerned about supervisors seeing their responses to sensitive questions, they might not be honest on a questionnaire. In that case, responses will not reflect true feelings. Validation evidence gives us some confidence that the instrument will reflect the satisfaction facets of interest. Finally, the use of an existing instrument saves the considerable cost and time necessary to develop an instrument from scratch.

The major disadvantage of using an existing instrument is that it will be limited to only those facets that the developers chose. The facets of most instruments tend to be general, which makes them applicable to most organizations. They will not include more specific areas of satisfaction or dissatisfaction that are issues for certain types of organizations or a particular organization. These could include satisfaction with specific decisions, events, individuals, or policies. One might want to assess, for example, satisfaction with the policy for rewarding people who are not absent from work. In a hospital one might wish to determine satisfaction with how employees are assigned to shifts, or with the quality assurance procedures.

Many existing instruments exist that can be used without charge for noncommercial educational and research purposes. For commercial uses there can be a fee. This book includes an appendix that contains a copy (Appendix Table A.1) and description of the Job Satisfaction Survey (JSS, Spector, 1985), which can be used and modified without fee for noncommercial educational and research purposes. Specific conditions and more information can be found on my website along with information about the commercial version, the JSS-2. URLs can be found in Appendix Table A.2.

Facet versus Global Instruments

A decision to be made in assessing job satisfaction is whether to assess only facets, only global satisfaction, or both. Some instruments assess facets, and as you will see, they vary in the number and nature of those included. Others measure only global or overall satisfaction. Sometimes facet instruments (e.g., the Job Satisfaction Survey, JSS) are used to assess global satisfaction by combining all the individual facet scores. There have been critics of this practice (Ironson, Smith, Brannick, Gibson, & Paul, 1989) who note that the sum of facets might not include all the factors that drive a person's global satisfaction. On the other hand Bowling and Zelazny (2021) did an in-depth comparison of facet versus global instruments, including several discussed in this chapter. They found that the facet and global instruments were highly correlated with one another, and that they related similarly to a variety of other variables. Although the sum of facets might not be a perfect substitute for a global instrument, it can be a close approximation.

This chapter will describe seven job satisfaction instruments, five that assess facets and two that assesses global satisfaction. Links to these instruments can be found in the assessment archive of my website (links are in Appendix Table A.2). The Job Satisfaction Survey (JSS, Spector, 1985), the Job Descriptive Index (JDI, Smith, Kendall, & Hulin, 1969), the Minnesota Satisfaction Questionnaire (MSQ, Weiss, Dawis, England, & Lofquist, 1967), and the Job Diagnostic Survey satisfaction subscales (JDS, Hackman & Oldham, 1975) are generic facet measures of job satisfaction that assess specific aspects of the job. The Job Satisfaction of Persons with Disabilities Scale (Brooks et al., 2021) is a two-facet instrument for a specialized population. The two general job satisfaction instruments are the Job in General Scale (JIG, Ironson et al., 1989), and the Michigan Organizational Assessment Questionnaire satisfaction subscale (MOAQ, Cammann, Fichman, Jenkins, & Klesh, 1979).

Other job satisfaction instruments have been developed besides the seven discussed here. More than 20 are described in Dail Fields (2002) guide to organizational measures. Many consulting firms have their own instruments that they use when hired to conduct surveys. For example, the Gallup Organization, perhaps the most widely known polling company, will conduct such surveys using their own or custom-made instruments.

Table 2.1 Facets from the Job Satisfaction Survey

Facet	Description
Pay	Salary and raises
Promotion	Opportunities for advancement in the organization
Supervision	The immediate supervisor
Fringe benefits	Insurance, leave and other benefits
Contingent rewards	Rewards given for good performance
Operating conditions	Rules and procedures
Coworkers	Peers at work
Nature of Work	The type of work done
Communication	How well management keeps employees informed

Job Satisfaction Survey (JSS)

The Job Satisfaction Survey (JSS, Spector, 1985) assesses nine facets of job satisfaction, as well as global satisfaction. Table 2.1 lists the nine facets, along with a brief description of each. The instrument contains 36 items and uses a summated rating scale format in which people indicate their agreement or disagreement with each item. This format is the most popular for job satisfaction instruments. Each of the nine facet subscales contain four items, and a total satisfaction score can be computed by combining all 36 items.

A copy of the instrument in the original English is in Appendix Table A.1 and copies in more than two dozen languages can be found on my website (web links are in Appendix Table A.2). Each of the items is a statement that is either favorable or unfavorable about an aspect of the job. The first item, for example, concerns pay, the second concerns promotion opportunities, etc. Respondents are asked to choose one of six response choices that corresponds to their agreement or disagreement about each item.

Scoring of the Job Satisfaction Survey

The JSS can yield ten scores. Each of the nine subscales can produce a separate facet score. The sum of all items (or all facets) produces a total global score. Each of the nine JSS subscales is scored by combining responses to its four items. Table 2.2 indicates which items go into each subscale. It also indicates which items need to be reverse scored, as will be explained below.

Table 2.2 Subscale Contents for the Job Satisfaction Survey

Subscale	Item Number
Pay	1, 10r, 19r, 28
Promotion	2r, 11, 20, 33
Supervision	3, 12r, 21r, 30
Fringe benefits	4r, 3, 22, 29r
Contingent rewards	5, 14r, 23r, 32r
Operating conditions	6r, 15, 24r, 31r
Coworkers	7, 16r, 25, 34r
Nature of work	8r, 17, 27, 35
Communication	9, 18r, 26r, 36r

Note: Items followed by "r" should be reverse scored.

To compute scores, responses to the individual items need to be added together. The responses to the JSS items are numbered from 1 (strongest disagreement) to 6 (strongest agreement), so respondents can have a score from 1 to 6 for each item. However, some of the items are scored in a positive and some in a negative direction. A positively worded item is one for which agreement indicates job satisfaction. The first item in the instrument, "I feel I am being paid a fair amount for the work I do" is positively worded. A negatively worded item is one for which agreement indicates dissatisfaction. Item number 10, "Raises are too few and far between" is negatively worded. Before the items are combined, the scoring for the negatively worded items must be reversed. Thus, people who agree with positively worded items and disagree with negatively worded items will have high scores representing satisfaction. People who disagree with positively worded items and agree with negatively worded items will have low scores representing dissatisfaction. Without item reversals, most respondents will have middle scores because they will tend to agree with half and disagree with half of the items, just because they are worded in opposite directions.

To reverse the scoring, you renumber the negatively worded item responses from 6 to 1 rather than 1 to 6. The response "disagree very much" becomes a 6 rather than a 1. The response "agree very much" becomes a 1 rather than a 6. Likewise, "disagree moderately" becomes a 5 rather than a 2 and "agree moderately" becomes a 2 rather than a 5. "Disagree slightly" is scored 4 rather than 3 and "agree slightly" is scored 3 rather than 4. An easy way to reverse score an item is to subtract respondent scores on the item from the sum of the lowest and highest possible responses. For example, with the JSS subtract each item from the sum of 1 and 6, which is equal to 7. This can easily be done with the standard statistical software such as JASP, R, SAS, or SPSSX. An expression that shows the item reversal for an item labeled ITEM2 is the following:

$$ITEM2 = 7 - ITEM2.$$

After the items are reversed, the numbered responses for the appropriate items are summed. The total satisfaction score is the sum of all 36 items. Individual facet scores are computed by summing the appropriate four items. Since each item's score can range from 1 to 6, the individual facet scores can range from 4 to 24. The lowest score is the sum of four ones, and the highest score is the sum of four sixes. The score for total satisfaction can range from 36 to 216. More detailed scoring instructions are on my website (see Appendix Table A.2 for the link).

Reliability

Two types of reliability estimates are important for evaluating an instrument. First, internal consistency reliability estimates refer to how well items of an instrument relate to one another. High internal consistency suggests that the items reflect the same underlying variable. Table 2.3 shows internal consistencies, or coefficient alphas, from a sample of 3,067 individuals who completed the JSS. These coefficient alphas ranged from 0.60 for the coworker subscale, to 0.91 for the total instrument. As noted earlier, the widely accepted internal consistency minimum for academic research is 0.70 (Nunnally, 1978), so the coworker subscale is somewhat lower than researchers like to see. The JSS-2 improves on the JSS in this regard with coefficient alphas all exceeding 0.90, so it is more suited for practitioner projects. Furthermore, it is not unusual for translated instruments to have somewhat lower coefficient alphas than their original language versions, as some items might not retain the precise nuance of meaning in a new language. The JSS is no exception, and some translations have yielded lower internal consistencies for some subscales. This is true, for example, of Chinese (Chou, Fu, Kröger, & Ru-Yan, 2011), Greek (Tsounis & Sarafis, 2018), and Spanish (Marion-Landais, 1993) translations.

Second, test-retest reliability indicates the stability of the instrument over time. Reliability data are available for the JSS from only one small

Table 2.3 Internal Consistency Reliability for the Job Satisfaction Survey

Subscale	Coefficient Alpha	Test-Retest Reliability
Pay	0.75	0.45
Promotion	0.73	0.62
Supervision	0.82	0.55
Benefits	0.73	0.37
Contingent rewards	0.76	0.59
Operating procedures	0.62	0.74
Coworkers	0.60	0.64
Nature of work	0.78	0.54
Communication	0.71	0.65
Total	0.91	0.71
Sample size	2870	43

Note: Test-retest reliability was assessed over an 18-month time span.

sample of 43 employees. These reliabilities, shown in Table 2.3, ranged from 0.37 to 0.74. The relative stability of satisfaction is remarkable in this sample, since the time span was 18 months during which several major changes occurred. These included a reorganization, layoffs, and a change of top administration. The stability of job satisfaction over time will be discussed further in Chapter 5 when we cover the dispositional nature of job attitudes.

Validity

Validity evidence for job satisfaction instruments is provided by comparing them to other job satisfaction instruments as well as with measures of other variables to which they would be expected to relate in theory. For example, five of the JSS subscales (pay, promotion, supervision, coworkers, and nature of work) correlate well with corresponding subscales of the JDI (Smith et al., 1969). These correlations ranged from 0.61 for coworkers to 0.80 for supervision.

The JSS has also been shown to correlate with many variables which we would expect to relate to job satisfaction. These include job characteristics as assessed with the Job Diagnostic Survey (Hackman & Oldham, 1975), age, organization level, absence, organizational commitment, leadership practices, intention to quit the job, and turnover (Spector, 1985).

Table 2.4 American Norms for the Job Satisfaction Survey

Subscale	Mean	Standard Deviation Across Samples
Pay	11.1	2.8
Promotion	11.9	1.8
Supervision	18.8	1.7
Benefits	14.0	2.1
Contingent rewards	13.1	1.8
Operating procedures	13.1	2.0
Coworkers	17.9	1.4
Nature of work	19.0	1.8
Communication	14.0	1.9
Total	134.8	21.6

Note: Norms based on 36,380 individuals from 136 samples. Mean is weighted mean which is the mean of all people who took the JSS (n = 36,380). Standard deviation is among sample means (n = 136).

Norms

Overall U.S. norms for the JSS are shown in Table 2.4 (more extensive norms are on my website; see links in Appendix Table A.2). The table shows the mean subscale and total job satisfaction scores across many employees and many samples. The table indicates the number of samples, as well as the total number of employees. Most samples represented a single organization, although several represent two or more organizations.

Job Descriptive Index (JDI)

The Job Descriptive Index (JDI, Smith et al., 1969) is a facet instrument that has been popular with academic researchers for decades. The instrument assesses five facets that each produce a separate score:

- Coworkers
- Pay
- Promotion
- Supervision
- Work

Many users of the JDI have summed the five facet scores into an overall score, although this practice is not recommended by Smith and her associates (Ironson et al., 1989). The instrument was updated in 1990 with the introduction of the global Job In General Scale that I discuss below (Balzer et al., 1990).

The entire instrument contains 72 items with either 9 or 18 items per subscale. Each item is an evaluative adjective or short phrase that is descriptive of the job. Responses are "yes", "uncertain", or "no". For each facet subscale, a brief explanation is provided, followed by the items concerning that facet. Both favorable or positively worded, and unfavorable or negatively worded items are provided. Three example items from the Work subscale are in Table 2.5.

There is an extensive body of literature in which the instrument has been used in academic research. In their meta-analysis of JDI validity, Kinicki, McKee-Ryan, Schriesheim, and Carson (2002) located 210 studies that used it, providing good validation evidence. The list would be longer today, although in more recent years the use of the JDI in published studies has declined. Extensive normative data are available for potential users of the instrument. The subscales also have good reliabilities with coefficient alphas in the 0.80s (Kinicki et al., 2002). Perhaps the biggest limitation of the JSS is that it contains only five facets whereas other instruments include more. In addition there has been some criticism that particular items might not apply to all employee groups (Buffum & Konick, 1982; Cook, Hepworth, Wall, & Warr, 1981).

Table 2.5 Sample Items from the Job Descriptive Index (JDI) Work Subscale

Think of the work you do at present. How well does each of the following words or phrases describe your work? In the blank beside each word below, write

__Y__ for "Yes" if it describes your work
__N__ for "No" if it does NOT describe it
__?__ if you cannot decide

Work on present job

_____ Routine
_____ Satisfying
_____ Good

Note. From Smith, Kendall, and Hulin (1969).

Potential users should be aware that the JDI is copyrighted, but it can be used free of charge for noncommercial educational and research purposes. A link to the Bowling Green University website for details can be found in the Job Attitude Measures section of my assessment archive (see Appendix Table A.2).

Minnesota Satisfaction Questionnaire (MSQ)

The Minnesota Satisfaction Questionnaire (MSQ, Weiss et al., 1967) is another satisfaction instrument that has been popular among academic researchers. The MSQ comes in two forms, a 100-item long version and a 20-item short form. It covers 20 facets, many of which are more specific than other satisfaction instruments. The long form contains five items per facet while the short form contains one. Most researchers who use the short form combine all the items into a single global score or compute separate extrinsic and intrinsic satisfaction subscales from subsets of items. Extrinsic satisfaction concerns aspects of work that have little to do with the job tasks or work itself, such as pay. Intrinsic satisfaction refers to the nature of job tasks themselves and how people feel about the work they do. If the 20 facets are of interest, it would be better to use the long version because multi-item subscales will have better reliability than single items.

The 20 facets of the Minnesota Satisfaction Questionnaire are listed in Table 2.6. As can be seen, the facets are in many cases more specific than the JDI or JSS. For example, satisfaction with supervision is divided into an interpersonal or human relations component and a technical competence component. The nature of work itself is reflected in several facets, including ability utilization, achievement, activity, creativity, independence, and variety. Despite the greater specificity of the MSQ facets, much of its content is contained in other instruments. For example, the JSS supervision items tap both the human relations and technical competence aspects.

For the MSQ short form, several studies have shown acceptable internal consistency reliabilities for the extrinsic, intrinsic, and total scores. Some researchers have questioned if the content of the extrinsic and intrinsic subscales are really distinct (Cook et al., 1981; Schriesheim, Powers, Scandura, Gardiner, & Lankau, 1993). The lack of clear discriminability of the subscales

Table 2.6 Facets from the Minnesota Satisfaction Questionnaire (MSQ)

Activity
Independence
Variety
Social status
Supervision (human relations)
Supervision (technical)
Moral values
Security
Social service
Authority
Ability utilization
Company policies and practices
Compensation
Advancement
Responsibility
Creativity
Working conditions
Coworkers
Recognition
Achievement

Note. From Weiss et al. (1967).

is reflected in the rather high correlations between them found in several studies (e.g., r = 0.83 in Schmitt, Coyle, White, & Rauchschenberger, 1978; r = 0.63 in Wexley, Alexander, Greenawalt, & Couch, 1980). Arvey and his associates (Arvey, Dewhirst, & Brown, 1978; Zultowski, Arvey, & Dewhirst, 1978) have devised an alternative scoring scheme for the two subscales.

One question with the long form concerns the discriminability of some subscales. Many are highly intercorrelated suggesting that they may be assessing the same (or highly related) aspects of the job. For example, the two supervision subscales were reported to correlate from 0.67 to 0.90 across samples by Weiss et al. (1967). Although we might wish to distinguish these two dimensions, employees might tend to feel the same about both aspects of their supervisors. On the positive side, corresponding subscales of the JDI and MSQ show good convergence (Gillet & Schwab, 1975).

One further note is that the MSQ is copyrighted, but it can be used free of charge for noncommercial educational and research purposes. A link to the University of Minnesota website to access the MSQ is in the Job Attitude Measures section of my online assessment archive (see Appendix Table A.2).

Table 2.7 Sample Items from the Job Diagnostic Survey Job Satisfaction Subscales

Facet	Item
Growth	The feeling of worthwhile accomplishment I get from doing my job.
Pay	The amount of pay and fringe benefits I receive.
Security	The amount of job security I have.
Social	The people I talk to and work with on my job.
Supervisor	The degree of respect and fair treatment I receive from my boss.
General	Most people on this job are very satisfied with the job.

Note. From Hackman and Oldham (1975).

Job Diagnostic Survey (JDS)

The Job Diagnostic Survey (JDS, Hackman & Oldham, 1975) is an instrument that was developed to study the effects of job characteristics on employees. It contains subscales to measure the nature of the job and job tasks, motivation, personality, psychological states (cognitions and feelings about job tasks), and job satisfaction. The JDS is discussed here as a facet measure because it covers several areas of job satisfaction, specifically growth, pay, security, social, and supervision, as well as global satisfaction.

The individual subscales contain from two to five items each. The format for the facet items is a 7-point scale ranging from "extremely dissatisfied" to "extremely satisfied". The format for the global satisfaction subscale is a 7-point ranging from "disagree strongly" to "agree strongly". Considering that its purpose was to study job characteristics, the JDS includes those facets that the authors felt were most important for this purpose. Sample items for each facet are in Table 2.7. A link to the scale is in the Attitude Measures section of my assessment archive (see Appendix Table A.2).

Job Satisfaction of Persons with Disabilities Scale

A job satisfaction instrument designed for a specific population is the Job Satisfaction of Persons with Disabilities Scale (Brooks et al., 2021). As the name implies, the purpose of the instrument was to assess job satisfaction of people who have mental health conditions. Although items ask about many of the same things as other job satisfaction instruments (e.g., pay, nature of work), many of the items deal with feeling accepted (e.g., "my coworkers accept me"). The instrument was developed in a mental health setting, but the items would be applicable to individuals with physical disabilities, as well.

Brooks et al. (2021) used factor analysis to derive two subscales that assess satisfaction with intangible benefits (nine items) and tangible benefits (five items). All items are written in a positive direction (high scores represent satisfaction), so items are summed into subscale scores. A link to the scale is in the Job Attitude Measures section of my online assessment archive (see Appendix Table A.2).

Job in General Scale (JIG)

The Job in General Scale (JIG, Ironson et al., 1989) was designed to assess global job satisfaction rather than facets (see sample items in Table 2.8). Its format is the same as the JDI, and it contains 18 items. Each item is an adjective or short phrase about the job in general rather than a facet. The total score is a combination of all items. Ironson et al. (1989) argue that overall job satisfaction is not the sum of individual facets, and that it should be assessed with a global instrument like the JIG.

As with the JDI, the JIG uses three response choices. For each item respondents are asked if they agree (yes), aren't sure (?) or disagree (no). Negatively worded items are reverse scored, and the total score is the sum of the responses.

The JIG has good internal consistency reliability. Ironson et al. (1989) reported internal consistency coefficients from 0.91 to 0.95 across several

Table 2.8 Three Items from the Job in General Scale (JIG)

Think of your job in general. All in all, what is it like most of the time? In the blank beside each word or phrase below, write

__Y__ for "Yes" if it describes your job
__N__ for "No" if it does NOT describe it
__?__ if you cannot decide

Job In General

_____ Undesirable
_____ Better than most
_____ Rotten

Note. From Ironson, Smith, Brannick, Gibson, and Paul (1989).

samples. They also noted that the JIG correlates well with other global measures of job satisfaction. The JIG would be an option for the assessment of global job satisfaction when this is of interest rather than facets. A link to the scale can be found in the Job Attitude Measures section of my online assessment archive (see Appendix Table A.2).

Michigan Organizational Assessment Questionnaire (MOAQ)

The Michigan Organizational Assessment Questionnaire (MOAQ, Cammann et al., 1979) contains a three-item overall job satisfaction subscale. The subscale is simple and short (three items), which makes it ideal for use in questionnaires that contain many subscales. Despite its short length, the subscale has good internal consistency. In a meta-analysis of 79 studies Bowling & Hammond (2008) found a mean internal consistency reliability of 0.84. The items of the instrument are shown in Table 2.9.

The original subscale used seven response choices "Strongly disagree", "Disagree", "Slightly disagree", "Neither agree nor disagree", "Slightly agree", "Agree", and "Strongly agree". Many who have used the MOAQ have changed to a 5-point or 6-point agreement scale. The responses are numbered from lowest to highest; with a 7-point scale this means 1 to 7, but the second item is reverse scored. The items are totaled to yield a global job satisfaction score. Validity evidence for the instrument is provided by research in which it has been correlated with many other work variables. Bowling et al.'s meta-analysis found the MOAQ to correlate significantly with more than three dozen variables. A link to the scale can be found in the Job Attitude Measures section of my online assessment archive (see Appendix Table A.2).

Table 2.9 Items from the Michigan Organizational Assessment Questionnaire Satisfaction Subscale

---

1. All in all I am satisfied with my job.
2. In general, I don't like my job.
3. In general, I like working here.

Note: From Cammann, Fichman, Jenkins, and Klesh (1979).

Developing or Modifying a Job Satisfaction Instrument

Often existing instruments cannot be found to assess the job satisfaction facets one wishes to assess. Under those circumstances one must develop a new instrument or modify an existing one. Although a detailed treatment of this topic is beyond the scope of this book, I will briefly note the basic steps involved in instrument development. Details can be found in other sources, such as DeVellis (1991) and Spector (1992). One must be careful that appropriate permissions are acquired before modifying copyrighted instruments. Although the procedure might seem relatively simple, it is best to consult an expert in psychological measurement the first time an instrument development project is undertaken to oversee the procedures that are used.

All the instruments discussed in this book used multiple items as opposed to single items. While the short form of the MSQ has a single item per facet, the items are combined into multiple item subscales. If one is interested in several facets, this can result in rather long instruments. It is reasonable to ask about the disadvantages of using a single-item instrument or subscale.

There are two good reasons to use multiple items. First, and most importantly, multiple item instruments are more reliable than single items. This is because respondents can make mistakes when filling out questionnaires. Errors can be produced when a respondent interprets a question differently than intended. For example, the question "I like my boss" might be intended to refer to the immediate supervisor, but some individuals might assume it refers to the top-level manager of the organization. In other cases, a person might misread an item. A common error is for a person to miss a "not" in an item. For example, the item "I do not like my pay" might be seen as "I do like my pay". Individuals also can interpret the item correctly but make a mistake and indicate the wrong response. For example, a person might mean to indicate "agree strongly" and mistakenly click the 1 instead of the 6. Mistakes that occur randomly across people can produce inconsistencies in scores for the same people over time. A person who mistakenly scores high on one occasion might correctly score low on another.

The larger the number of items in a subscale, the smaller the effect of inconsistent responses to items over time. With a single item, an error can move a person's score from one end of the scale to the other. With multiple items an error can only move a person's score a portion of the total range of scores. With ten items, each item contributes only 10% of the total score. This produces more stability in scores over time, and hence more reliability.

Second, multiple items allow for a more complete assessment of a facet. What may seem to be a simple facet can have several aspects to it. A single item may not do a good job of covering all aspects. For example, a person may be able to indicate their overall satisfaction with pay in a single item but pay includes many aspects which would take several items to cover. There is the amount of pay, size of raises, frequency of raises, fairness of pay policies, sufficiency to meet financial needs, prospects for future increases, and connection to performance. An individual who answers a single item might do so in response to only some of these aspects. Multiple items allow for more specific questions and allow for the more complete assessment of the facet.

Of course, there are times when multiple items are not feasible due to overall questionnaire length. In those cases a single-item measure, though not ideal, can be a reasonable compromise between measurement rigor and practical limitations (Wanous, Reichers, & Hudy, 1997).

Procedure for Instrument Development

The complete development of a satisfaction instrument is a five-step process. Table 2.10 lists the steps involved in such an undertaking. The first step is to precisely define the facet or facets of interest. It is here that many instrument development efforts are compromised because the exact nature of the construct of interest was left ambiguous and incompletely described. There are two major ways in which a facet can be delineated and developed. First, the instrument developers can consult their own experience or the research literature to define the various aspects of a facet. Second, interviews with employees can be conducted to help define the various aspects. When an instrument is developed for use in a particular organization, it is not uncommon to interview a sample of employees from that organization to help precisely define the facets of interest.

Once the facets are clearly defined, items can be written to assess them. If a facet has multiple aspects to it, multiple items can be written to cover them. The better and more thorough the job done on defining the facet, the easier it will be to write items. A good item is a clear, concise, concrete statement that reflects either something favorable or unfavorable about a job or an

Table 2.10 Five Steps for Developing a Satisfaction Scale

Five Steps for Developing a Satisfaction Scale	
Step 1	Carefully and thoroughly define the facet
Step 2	Design scale format and write items
Step 3	Pilot test items on small sample
Step 4	Administer items to large sample and item analyze
Step 5	Compile norms and validation evidence on multiple samples

aspect of the job. Part of the item generation step is to choose a format for the instrument. For example, will the instrument have the checklist look of the JDI or the summated rating scale format of the MSQ?

The third step is to administer the new items to a small sample to pilot test them. The purpose of this is to be sure that the items are clear and understandable. The fourth step is to administer the instrument to a sample and conduct an item analysis. An item analysis is a statistical procedure that is used to determine the items that work best from the perspective of internal consistency reliability. This means that items are chosen that intercorrelate well with one another. A statistic called the item-remainder correlation is computed for each item to show how well it relates to the sum of all other items. Coefficient alpha is an indication of how well the various items relate to one another and form an internally consistent instrument.

The final step is to collect validation evidence and compile norms. This last step is one that is often skipped when instruments are developed for practice uses in organizations. This is because it can be quite difficult and time-consuming to conduct validation studies. It is a requirement for publication of academic research papers about the development of new job satisfaction or other instruments. Validation is always a good idea, however, to demonstrate that the interpretation of results is reasonable. Unfortunately, constraints when conducting practitioner projects often do not allow for this to be done.

Translating Job Satisfaction Instruments

The job satisfaction instruments discussed in this chapter, like the JSS, were written in English and developed on native English-speakers. They are sometimes translated into other languages to be used by academic researchers or practitioners. To be used most effectively, job satisfaction instruments must be carefully translated, and psychometric properties checked, as there is no guarantee that a new instrument will work as intended. Ideally this involves back-translation and a check of measurement equivalence/invariance or ME/I (Spector, Liu, & Sanchez, 2015).

Back-translation is a two-step process in which one bilingual person translates the instrument from the source language (e.g., English) to the target language (e.g., Spanish). Then a second bilingual person independently back-translates from the target (e.g., Spanish) back to the source language (e.g., English). In the best case, a person who is a native speaker of the source language compares the original source with the back-translation to be sure the meaning has not changed. Feedback is given to the two translators so they can fix discrepancies. A back-translation procedure can assure equivalence of meaning between source and target versions of the instrument, but it cannot assure that the items will work together as planned. The internal consistency can suffer as the translated items might not have the same connotations as the originals or might have different interpretations due to cultural differences.

ME/I can be tested by comparing results of at least two samples, one using the instrument in the source language and the other in the target language. Ideally, the two samples would be matched as closely as possible on occupation and organization type. For example, samples of hospital nurses for both samples would be a reasonable match. Comparing hospital nurses in one sample and corporate accountants in another would not be, as it would be impossible to know if differences were due to language and culture or to occupation.

Conducting an ME/I analysis involves complex statistics (Spector et al., 2015), with two major approaches based on either item response theory (IRT) or structural equation modeling (SEM). The complexities are beyond the scope here (for an overview, see Spector et al., 2015), but both approaches investigate the interrelationships among the items in the assessment. They show that interrelationships among the items are similar between the two samples, and therefore demonstrate measurement equivalence.

References

Arvey, R. D., Dewhirst, H. D., & Brown, E. M. (1978). A longitudinal study of the impact of changes in goal setting on employee satisfaction. *Personnel Psychology, 31,* 595–608. doi: 10.1111/j.1744-6570.1978.tb00465.x

Balzer, W. K., Smith, P. C., Kravitz, D. E., Lovell, S. E., Paul, K. B., Reilly, B. A., & Reilly, C. E. (1990). *User's manual for the Job Descriptive Index (JDI) and* the Job in General (JIG) scales. Bowling Green, OH: Bowling Green State University.

Barling, J., & Macewen, K. E. (1988). A multitrait-multimethod analysis of four maternal employment role experiences. *Journal of Organizational Behavior, 9*, 335–344. doi: 10.1002/job.4030090405

Bowling, N. A., & Hammond, G. D. (2008). A meta-analytic examination of the construct validity of the Michigan Organizational Assessment Questionnaire Job Satisfaction Subscale. *Journal of Vocational Behavior, 73*, 63–77. doi: 10.1016/j.jvb.2008.01.004

Bowling, N. A., & Zelazny, L. (2021). Measuring general job satisfaction: Which is more construct valid—global scales or facet-composite scales? *Journal of Business and Psychology.* doi: 10.1007/s10869-021-09739-2

Brooks, J. M., Iwanaga, K., Chan, F., Lee, B., Chen, X., Wu, J.-R., Walker, R., & Fortuna, K. L. (2021). Psychometric validation of the Job Satisfaction of Persons with Disabilities Scale in a sample of peer support specialists. *Psychiatric Rehabilitation Journal, 44*, 93–98. doi: 10.1037/prj0000411

Buffum, W. E., & Konick, A. (1982). Employees' job satisfaction, residents' functioning, and treatment progress in psychiatric institutions. *Health & Social Work, 7*, 320–327. doi: 10.1093/hsw/7.4.320

Cammann, C., Fichman, M., Jenkins, D., & Klesh, J. (1979). *The Michigan organizational assessment questionnaire.* Unpublished manuscript. Ann Arbor: University of Michigan.

Chou, Y.-C., Fu, L.-Y., Kröger, T., & Ru-Yan, C. (2011). Job satisfaction and quality of life among home care workers: a comparison of home care workers who are and who are not informal carers. *International Psychogeriatrics, 23*, 814–825. doi: 10.1017/s104161021000219x

Cook, J. D., Hepworth, S. J., Wall, T. D., & Warr, P. B. (1981). *The experience of work.* New York City: Academic Press.

DeVellis, R. F. (1991). *Scale development theory and applications.* Thousand Oaks, CA: Sage.

Fields, D. (2002). *Taking the measure of work.* Thousand Oaks, CA: Sage.

Gillet, B., & Schwab, D. P. (1975). Convergent and discriminant validities of corresponding Job Descriptive Index and Minnesota Satisfaction Questionnaire scales. *Journal of Applied Psychology, 60*, 313–317. doi: 10.1037/h0076751

Glick, W. H., Jenkins, G., & Gupta, N. (1986). Method versus substance: How strong are underlying relationships between job characteristics and attitudinal outcomes? *Academy of Management Journal, 29*, 441–464.

Hackman, J. R., & Oldham, G. R. (1975). Development of the Job Diagnostic Survey. *Journal of Applied Psychology, 60,* 159–170.

Ironson, G. H., Smith, P. C., Brannick, M. T., Gibson, W. M., & Paul, K. B. (1989). Construction of a Job in General scale: A comparison of global, composite, and specific measures. *Journal of Applied Psychology, 74,* 193–200. doi: 10.1037/0021-9010.74.2.193

Kinicki, A. J., McKee-Ryan, F. M., Schriesheim, C. A., & Carson, K. P. (2002). Assessing the construct validity of the Job Descriptive Index: A review and meta-analysis. *Journal of Applied Psychology, 87,* 14–32. doi: 10.1037/0021-9010.87.1.14

Marion-Landais, C. A. (1993). *A cross-cultural study of leader-member exchange quality and job satisfaction as correlates of intra-dyadic work-value congruence.* Tampa, FL: University of South Florida.

Nunnally, J. C. (1978). *Psychometric theory* (2nd ed.). New York: McGraw-Hill.

Schmitt, N., Coyle, B. W., White, J. K., & Rauchschenberger, J. (1978). Background, needs, job perceptions, and job satisfaction: A causal model. *Personnel Psychology, 31,* 889–901. doi: 10.1111/j.1744-6570.1978.tb02129.x

Schriesheim, C. A., Powers, K. J., Scandura, T. A., Gardiner, C. C., & Lankau, M. J. (1993). Improving construct measurement in management research: Comments and a quantitative approach for assessing the theoretical content adequacy of paper-and-pencil survey-type instruments. *Journal of Management, 19,* 385–417. doi: 10.1016/0149-2063(93)90058-U

Smith, P. C., Kendall, L. M., & Hulin, C. L. (1969). *Measurement of satisfaction in work and retirement.* Chicago: Rand McNally.

Spector, P. E. (1985). Measurement of human service staff satisfaction: Development of the Job Satisfaction Survey. *American Journal of Community Psychology, 13,* 693–713. doi: 10.1007/BF00929796

Spector, P. E. (1992). *Summated rating scale construction: An introduction.* Thousand Oaks, CA: Sage Publications, Inc.

Spector, P. E., Dwyer, D. J., & Jex, S. M. (1988). Relation of job stressors to affective, health, and performance outcomes: A comparison of multiple data sources. *Journal of Applied Psychology, 73,* 11–19. doi: 10.1037/0021-9010.73.1.11

Spector, P. E., Liu, C., & Sanchez, J. I. (2015). Methodological and substantive issues in conducting multinational and cross-cultural research. *Annual Review of Organizational Psychology and Organizational Behavior, 2,* 101–131. doi: 10.1146/annurev-orgpsych-032414-111310

Trice, A. D., & Tillapaugh, P. (1991). Children's estimates of their parents' job satisfaction. *Psychological Reports, 69,* 63–66. doi: 10.2466/pro.1991.69.1.63

Tsounis, A., & Sarafis, P. (2018). Validity and reliability of the Greek translation of the Job Satisfaction Survey (JSS). *BMC Psychology, 6,* 27. doi: 10.1186/s40359-018-0241-4

Wanous, J. P., Reichers, A. E., & Hudy, M. J. (1997). Overall job satisfaction: how good are single-item measures? *Journal of Applied Psychology, 82,* 247–252.

Weiss, D. J., Dawis, R. V., England, G. W., & Lofquist, L. H. (1967). *Manual for the Minnesota satisfaction questionnaire.* Minneapolis: University of Minnesota.

Wexley, K. N., Alexander, R. A., Greenawalt, J. P., & Couch, M. A. (1980). Attitudinal congruence and similarity as related to interpersonal evaluations in manager-subordinate dyads. *The Academy of Management Journal, 23,* 320–330. doi: 10.2307/255434

Zultowski, W. H., Arvey, R. D., & Dewhirst, H. D. (1978). Moderating effects of organizational climate on relationships between goal-setting attributes and employee satisfaction. *Journal of Vocational Behavior, 12,* 217–227. doi: 10.1016/0001-8791(78)90036-2

3

HOW PEOPLE FEEL ABOUT WORK

Every year the Gallup Organization conducts their Work and Education Poll to determine among other things how Americans feel about their jobs and issues related to employment. In the August 2020 poll, taken during the height of the COVID pandemic, Gallup found that satisfaction with safety at work showed a large drop from 74% satisfied in 2019 to 65% satisfied in 2020 (Jones, 2020). Other facets of satisfaction remained steady or even a little higher. These results show how job satisfaction can be affected by forces outside of the workplace.

Surveys conducted in the U.S. generally show that most Americans are satisfied with their jobs overall. A 2016 Pew Research Center poll found that most Americans were either very satisfied (49%) or somewhat satisfied (30%), with 15% saying they were dissatisfied (Pew Research Center, 2016). Feelings about the job are likely to vary across different countries, a topic I will discuss later.

The 2020 Gallup poll of Americans included a list of job facets. Figure 3.1 shows the percentage of Americans who indicated being satisfied with

DOI: 10.4324/9781003250616-3

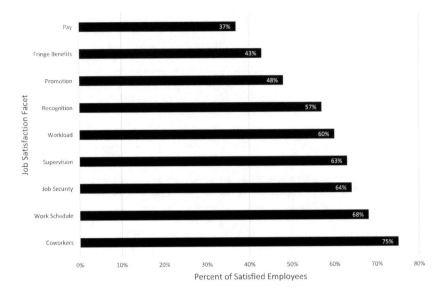

Figure 3.1 Percentage of Americans satisfied with job facets according to 2020 Gallup Poll. From Jones (2020).

each facet. As can be seen, most Americans are satisfied with recognition, workload, supervision, job security, work schedule, and coworkers in increasing order. The majority were not satisfied with rewards (pay, fringe benefits, and promotion opportunities).

The Gallup pattern of facet satisfaction can also be seen in the Job Satisfaction Survey (JSS) norms in Table 2.4. The typical American is satisfied with coworkers, nature of work itself, and supervision, but not very satisfied with rewards, such as fringe benefits and pay. Some of the reason for this might be that Americans tend to expect to advance at work and experience an increase in standard of living as a reward for hard work. Thus, they are often somewhat dissatisfied with their career and salary progress. The facet satisfaction patterns are not necessarily the same in all countries, as I will discuss in the section on cultural differences in job satisfaction.

Age

Research has shown that age and job satisfaction are related, but the exact form is not entirely clear. Some studies have found a linear relationship with satisfaction increasing with age (White & Spector, 1987). Others have found a curvilinear relationship with job satisfaction at first declining as people get older, but at a certain point reversing and increasing with age (Birdi, Warr, & Oswald, 1995; Clark, Oswald, & Warr, 1996). In these studies, job satisfaction hit the lowest level around age 26–31 and steadily increased after that.

A factor that might be important in the age-job satisfaction relationship is gender (Clark et al., 1996). Clark et al. surveyed over 5,000 men and women in a U.K. study. They found clear curvilinear relationships of age with global job satisfaction, as well as nature of work and pay facets for men. For women, the curvilinear pattern was of smaller magnitude for global job satisfaction and did not exist for either facet. Only a linear relation was found for women.

The Clark et al. (1996) study suggests that age distribution and gender composition of samples can affect whether or not the curvilinear pattern is detected. An adequate sample for this purpose should range in age from late teens to late 60s and contain few women. An additional factor that affects these tests is that analyses used to detect curvilinear relationships generally have lower statistical power than do procedures to detect linear patterns. Failure to find significant curvilinear trends might be caused in some cases by relatively low statistical power due to insufficient sample size rather than linearity (Bedeian, Ferris, & Kacmar, 1992).

Whether the relationship is curvilinear or linear, it is important to understand the reasons that age relates to job satisfaction. Several hypotheses have been advanced. Wright and Hamilton (1978) proposed two likely mechanisms. The cohort mechanism is that expectations and values of people, at least in Western countries, have changed over time. Older workers are more satisfied with their jobs than younger workers because they are more accepting of authority and expect less from their jobs. The job change mechanism is that due to experience and seniority older workers have better jobs and more skill than their younger counterparts. They are more satisfied because their jobs are more satisfying. There are two additional possibilities. First, that over time people have more "sunk costs" or investments in a job. Those investments in terms of benefits (e.g., pension), and rewards (e.g., pay) might contribute to job satisfaction. Second, over time people adapt to the job by adjusting their expectations to be more realistic, so that they are happier with less as they get older.

An adequate test of the cohort mechanism would require a long-term longitudinal study in which a sample of people would be assessed throughout life to see how their job satisfaction changed over time and what was associated with those changes. The job change mechanism has received at least some empirical support. White and Spector (1987) showed that the age-job satisfaction relationship could be explained by better job conditions for older workers. Older workers reported a closer match between what they had and what they wanted in terms of job conditions as well as higher salary. They also perceived a higher level of personal control over job rewards.

Another factor that affects the age-job satisfaction relationship is country. Drabe, Hauff, and Richter (2015) examined age and job satisfaction in Germany, Japan, and the U.S. They found that predictors of job satisfaction vary with country. For example, advancement opportunities and job security are related to job satisfaction in the U.S., but not Germany or Japan. Income was related to job satisfaction in the U.S., but not in Japan. Further, with age, what is important in a job changes, with older workers, compared to younger, putting more emphasis on good working relationships and less emphasis on pay and interesting work.

Country Differences

Comparisons have been made of the global job satisfaction of employees from different countries, although the number of countries compared has been limited. Figure 3.2 shows the mean job satisfaction in samples of managers from 24 countries (Spector et al., 2001). As can be seen, global satisfaction was highest in Canada and Sweden. East Asian samples were all near the bottom, but it should be kept in mind that there can be cultural differences in how people use rating scales. East Asians sometimes exhibit a modesty bias in avoiding the highest positive ratings about features of their jobs (Spector, Liu, & Sanchez, 2015). This bias could account for the differences rather than Asians being less satisfied. As noted by Sousa-Poza and Sousa-Poza (2000) in their comparison across 21 diverse countries, although there are some mean country differences, most employed people regardless of where they live are satisfied with their jobs.

There have been only a handful of country comparisons of job satisfaction facets using the same facet instrument. Table 3.1 shows results for the

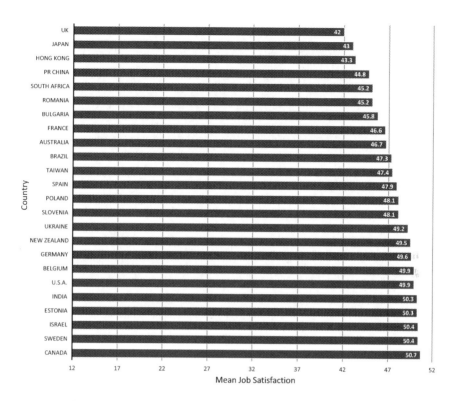

Figure 3.2 The mean global job satisfaction by country. From Spector et al. (2001).

JSS facet subscales plus the total global score across seven countries including the U.S. The countries could be placed into two groups according to global job satisfaction. The high group with scores over 150 consists of the Dominican Republic, Pakistan, and Taiwan. The low group with scores below 140 consists of Greece, Singapore, Turkey, and the U.S. The patterns across facets varied by country, as well. For example, in Greece, Pakistan, and the U.S., satisfaction was lowest among the facets for Pay. Promotion Opportunities had the lowest satisfaction in Singapore and Taiwan. In the Dominican Republic scores were over 16 for all facets but Operating Procedures, which was a 12.3. Pakistan had relatively little variation among facets, with all means between 16.9 (Pay) and 19.8 (Communication). Americans had relatively low scores for rewards (Pay, Promotion Opportunities, Fringe Benefits, and Contingent Rewards) and relatively high means for social aspects of work (Coworkers and Supervisions) and the nature of their work.

Table 3.1 Job Satisfaction Survey Facet Comparisons across Seven Countries

Facet	Dominican Republic[a]	Greece[b]	Pakistan[c]	Singapore[d]	Taiwan[e]	Turkey[f]	US[g]
Pay	17.2	9.5	16.9	14.0	15.0	11.9	11.1
Promotion	16.4	10.1	17.1	13.4	12.0	12.5	11.9
Supervision	20.0	16.6	19.3	13.4	19.9	17.3	18.8
Benefits	16.8	11.6	19.6	14.2	15.1	13.3	14.0
Contingent rewards	17.8	14.0	17.3	17.3	17.4	11.2	13.1
Procedures	12.3	13.1	17.0	17.0	15.6	15.7	13.1
Coworkers	20.0	18.1	19.5	13.4	20.2	18.1	17.9
Work	22.2	18.8	19.7	17.1	20.4	12.9	19.0
Communication	18.1	14.6	19.8	14.9	19.0	18.4	14.0
Total	160.9	128.3	157.0	134.7	154.5	157.2	134.8
Sample size	148	239	153	182	1,641	380	36,380

a   Marion-Landais (1993).
b   Tsounis and Sarafis (2018).
c   Shahzad and Begum (2011).
d   Spector and Wimalasiri (1986).
e   Chou, Fu, Kröger, and Ru-Yan (2011).
f   Yelboga (2009).
g   From JSS norms: https://paulspector.com/assessments/pauls-no-cost-assessments/job-satisfaction-survey-jss/job-satisfaction-survey-norm.

Although there are clearly country differences, it is difficult to draw firm conclusions from means that came from different studies. These studies have been conducted over time, and although they all used the same job satisfaction instrument, the samples were not all the same. For example, the Dominican sample consisted of locals working for an American telecom company. The Greek sample consisted of employees of a drug treatment facility. The Turkish sample came from employees in the financial industry. It is difficult to know the extent to which differences are due to country or the nature of the sample. Such sample industry and occupation differences can be seen in the American norms for the JSS comparing industries (Spector, 2021b), but those differences are not as large as those found among these countries. Biases can also be a factor in these studies. Marion-Landais (1993) argued that one reason for the high job satisfaction in his Dominican sample may have been that his subjects were fearful about expressing dissatisfaction. They may have inflated their job satisfaction ratings, to avoid seeming critical of their employer.

Gender

In their meta-analysis of gender and job satisfaction, Batz-Barbarich, Tay, Kuykendall, and Cheung (2018) compiled results of 264 studies involving more than 360,000 employed men and women. Despite having enough statistical power to detect even trivial differences, they found that men and women did not differ in job satisfaction. This lack of a job satisfaction difference between men and women despite assumed disadvantages women have (e.g., lower pay) has led to what some call the paradox of the contented female worker (Fernández Puente & Sánchez-Sánchez, 2021). That is, women should be less satisfied at work because their work experiences are less favorable than men.

Fernández Puente and Sánchez-Sánchez (2021) discuss three mechanisms that might explain why women are not less satisfied than men:

- Self-selection. Only the happiest and most motivated women choose to work, and thus they are predisposed to be satisfied.
- Flexibility. Women choose jobs that allow greater flexibility (e.g., in working hours) which enhances their satisfaction.
- Expectations. Women have lower expectations than men and are equally satisfied with less. In part this could be the result of women comparing themselves to other women rather than to men.

Research is needed to determine if any of these mechanisms is correct. However, it should be noted that societal level differences in things like mean levels of pay between men and women (the next chapter discusses how pay is not a major factor in job satisfaction) do not necessarily reflect the day-to-day working experiences of most women. Men and women might not differ in job satisfaction because their job experiences are not very different.

Another aspect of gender concerns the workplace experiences of transgender employees. Such employees are at risk for mistreatment at work and often need support by colleagues. Thoroughgood, Sawyer, and Webster (2021) surveyed 177 transgender employees about the support they received at work, focusing on oppositional courage. The employees indicated the extent to which coworkers had the courage to defend their transgender colleagues with others. This included advocating for transgender policies and speaking out when transgender colleagues were mistreated. For the transgender employees in the study, perceiving this sort of courageous support was associated with greater job satisfaction.

Racial Differences in the U.S.

Most of the job satisfaction research on ethnicity and race has focused on Black-White differences in the U.S. A meta-analysis by Koh, Shen, and Lee (2016) found a small difference (White employees had higher satisfaction) that was statistically significant with a sample size of more than 750,000. When they analyzed for type of job, Koh et al. found that Blacks were more satisfied than Whites with low complexity jobs and less satisfied with high complexity jobs. The reason for these results could not be determined from the meta-analysis, but they suggest that the connection between race and job satisfaction is complex.

One thing to keep in mind when interpreting Black-White differences is that there are racial differences in the jobs that people hold. For example, Tuch and Martin (1991) found in their nationally representative samples that Black workers were more likely to be in blue collar jobs, live in cities, and perceive fewer rewards at work. Somers and Birnbaum (2001) investigated whether there would be Black-White differences in job satisfaction when differences between the samples were controlled. They found that after controlling for age, education, and the type of work, there were no significant racial differences in job satisfaction.

Disabled Workers

Many workers have disabilities that affect the sorts of job tasks that they can perform. Disabilities can be physical (e.g., hearing impairment) or psychological (e.g., cognitive impairment). The type of impairment can create challenges that might affect job satisfaction. In a nationally representative sample of Americans, Brooks (2019) found that employees with disabilities have lower job satisfaction than their nondisabled colleagues. Much of the difference could be attributed to the disabled employees feeling a lack of respect by others at work.

Research on people with intellectual disability shows that they tend to be high on job satisfaction, and in some studies, are higher than counterparts without intellectual disability (Kocman & Weber, 2018). The authors noted in their review of studies in this area that people with intellectual disabilities are more satisfied when working in a regular community job rather than in a sheltered workshop. These findings fit well with those of Brooks (2019) that disabled employees are happy with job settings where they feel respected.

Neurodiversity

There is a growing trend to expanding workplace diversity by hiring people whose mental functioning is different due to what are often considered disorders like attention deficit hyperactive disorder (ADHD), autism, and learning disabilities (Krzeminska, Austin, Bruyère, & Hedley, 2019). The neurodiversity idea is that such differences are part of natural variation in how people process information, and that people who are neurodiverse can still be productive members of society. Such individuals can bring a variety of talents that make them valuable contributors to organizations (Krzeminska & Hawse, 2020). Neurodiverse employees, however, experience significant challenges in the workplace, which can be overcome in many cases by creating a working environment that is inclusive (Spector, 2021a).

Research on the job satisfaction of neurodiverse employees is limited. Hillier et al. (2007) followed a small group of people with autism as they began regular employment. Their job satisfaction was high (mean of 4 on a 5-point scale) which is not unlike that found in neurotypical (people who are not neurodiverse) samples. Hedley, Uljarević, Bury, and Dissanayake (2019) found that scores on autism trait severity in a sample of employees with autism was unrelated to job satisfaction. Further, their scores on the MSQ short form were quite close to the norms for the scale (Weiss, Dawis, England, & Lofquist, 1967), again suggesting that neurodiverse employees might not differ from neurotypical employees in job satisfaction.

References

Batz-Barbarich, C., Tay, L., Kuykendall, L., & Cheung, H. K. (2018). A meta-analysis of gender differences in subjective well-being: Estimating effect sizes and associations with gender inequality. *Psychological Science, 29*, 1491–1503. doi: 10.1177/0956797618774796

Bedeian, A. G., Ferris, G. R., & Kacmar, K. M. (1992). Age, tenure, and job satisfaction: A tale of two perspectives. *Journal of Vocational Behavior, 40*, 33–48. doi: 10.1016/0001-8791(92)90045-2

Birdi, K., Warr, P., & Oswald, A. (1995). Age differences in three components of employee well-being. *Applied Psychology: An International Review, 44*, 345–373. doi: 10.1111/j.1464-0597.1995.tb01085.x

Brooks, J. D. (2019). Just a little respect: Differences in job satisfaction among individuals with and without disabilities. *Social Science Quarterly, 100*, 379–388. doi: 10.1111/ssqu.12543

Chou, Y.-C., Fu, L.-Y., Kröger, T., & Ru-Yan, C. (2011). Job satisfaction and quality of life among home care workers: a comparison of home care workers who are and who are not informal carers. *International Psychogeriatrics, 23*, 814–825. doi: 10.1017/s104161021000219x

Clark, A., Oswald, A., & Warr, P. (1996). Is job satisfaction U-shaped in age? *Journal of Occupational and Organizational Psychology, 69*, 57–81.

Drabe, D., Hauff, S., & Richter, N. F. (2015). Job satisfaction in aging workforces: An analysis of the USA, Japan and Germany. *The International Journal of Human Resource Management, 26*, 783–805. doi: 10.1080/09585192.2014.939101

Fernández Puente, A. C., & Sánchez-Sánchez, N. (2021). How gender-based disparities affect women's job satisfaction? Evidence from euro-area. *Social Indicators Research*. doi: 10.1007/s11205-021-02647-1

Hedley, D., Uljarević, M., Bury, S. M., & Dissanayake, C. (2019). Predictors of mental health and well-being in employed adults with autism spectrum disorder at 12-month follow-up. *Autism Research, 12*, 482–494. doi: 10.1002/aur.2064

Hillier, A., Campbell, H., Mastriani, K., Izzo, M. V., Kool-Tucker, A. K., Cherry, L., & Beversdorf, D. Q. (2007). Two-year evaluation of a vocational support program for adults on the autism spectrum. *Career Development for Exceptional Individuals, 30*, 35–47. doi: 10.1177/08857288070300010501

Jones, J. M. (2020). U.S. worker satisfaction with job safety down amid COVID. Retrieved from https://news.gallup.com/poll/309188/worker-satisfaction-job-safety-down-amid-covid.aspx

Kocman, A., & Weber, G. (2018). Job satisfaction, quality of work life and work motivation in employees with intellectual disability: A systematic review. *Journal of Applied Research in Intellectual Disabilities, 31*, 1–22. doi: 10.1111/jar.12319

Koh, C. W., Shen, W., & Lee, T. (2016). Black–White mean differences in job satisfaction: A meta-analysis. *Journal of Vocational Behavior, 94*, 131–143. doi: 10.1016/j.jvb.2016.02.009

Krzeminska, A., Austin, R. D., Bruyère, S. M., & Hedley, D. (2019). The advantages and challenges of neurodiversity employment in organizations. *Journal of Management & Organization, 25*, 453–463. doi: 10.1017/jmo.2019.58

Krzeminska, A., & Hawse, S. (2020). *Mainstreaming neurodiversity for an inclusive and sustainable future workforce: Autism-spectrum employees* (pp. 229–261). Singapore: Springer.

Marion-Landais, C. A. (1993). *A cross-cultural study of leader-member exchange quality and job satisfaction as correlates of intra-dyadic work-value congruence.* : Tampa: University of South Florida.

Pew Research Center. (2016). The state of American jobs: 3. How Americans view their jobs, from https://www.pewresearch.org/social-trends/2016/10/06/3-how-americans-view-their-jobs/

Shahzad, S., & Begum, N. (2011). Urdu translation and psychometric properties of Job Satisfaction Survey (JSS) in Pakistan. *The International Journal of Educational and Psychological Assessment, 9*, 57–74.

Somers, M. J., & Birnbaum, D. (2001). Racial differences in work attitudes: What you see depends on what you study. *Journal of Business and Psychology, 15*, 579–591. doi: 10.1023/A:1007818917086

Sousa-Poza, A., & Sousa-Poza, A. A. (2000). Well-being at work: a cross-national analysis of the levels and determinants of job satisfaction. *The Journal of Socio-Economics, 29*, 517–538. doi: 10.1016/S1053-5357(00)00085-8

Spector, P. E. (2021a). How to build a neurodiversity climate for your company. Retrieved from https://paulspector.com/how-to-build-a-neurodiverity-climate-for-your-company/

Spector, P. E. (2021b). Job satisfaction survey norms, from https://paulspector.com/assessments/pauls-no-cost-assessments/job-satisfaction-survey-jss/job-satisfaction-survey-norms/

Spector, P. E., Cooper, C. L., Sanchez, J. I., O'Driscoll, M., Sparks, K., Bernin, P., Bussing, A., Dewe, P., Hart, P. M., Lu, L., Miller, K., De Moraes, L. F. R., Ostrognay, G. M., Pagon, M., Pitariu, H., Poelmans, S., Radhakrishnan, P., Russinova, V., Salamatov, V., Salgado, J., Shima, S., Siu, O. L., Stora, J. B., Teichmann, M., Theorell, T., Vlerick, P., Westman, M., Widerszal-Bazyl, M., Wong, P., & Yu, S. (2001). Do national levels of individualism and internal locus of control relate to well-being: An ecological level international study. *Journal of Organizational Behavior, 22*, 815–832. doi: 10.1002/job.118

Spector, P. E., Liu, C., & Sanchez, J. I. (2015). Methodological and substantive issues in conducting multinational and cross-cultural research. *Annual Review of Organizational Psychology and Organizational Behavior, 2*, 101–131. doi: 10.1146/annurev-orgpsych-032414-111310

Spector, P. E., & Wimalasiri, J. (1986). A cross-cultural comparison of job satisfaction dimensions in the United States and Singapore. *International Review of Applied Psychology, 35*, 147–158. doi: 10.1111/j.1464-0597.1986.tb00909.x

Thoroughgood, C. N., Sawyer, K. B., & Webster, J. R. (2021). Because you're worth the risks: Acts of oppositional courage as symbolic messages of relational value to transgender employees. *Journal of Applied Psychology, 106*, 399–421. doi: 10.1037/apl0000515.supp (Supplemental)

Tsounis, A., & Sarafis, P. (2018). Validity and reliability of the Greek translation of the Job Satisfaction Survey (JSS). *BMC Psychology, 6*, 27.

Tuch, S. A., & Martin, J. K. (1991). Race in the workplace. *The Sociological Quarterly, 32*, 103–116. doi: 10.1111/j.1533-8525.1991.tb00347.x

Weiss, D. J., Dawis, R. V., England, G. W., & Lofquist, L. H. (1967). *Manual for the Minnesota satisfaction questionnaire*. Minneapolis: University of Minnesota.

White, A., & Spector, P. E. (1987). An investigation of age-related factors in the age-job-satisfaction relationship. *Psychology and Aging, 2*, 261–265. doi: 10.1037/0882-7974.2.3.261

Wright, J. D., & Hamilton, R. F. (1978). Work satisfaction and age: Some evidence for the 'job change' hypothesis. *Social Forces, 56*, 1140–1158. doi: 10.2307/2577515

Yelboga, A. (2009). Validity and reliability of the Turkish version of the Job Satisfaction Survey (JSS). *World Applied Sciences Journal, 6*, 1066–1072.

4

ENVIRONMENTAL AND JOB FACTORS

There are a wide range of environmental factors that are associated with job satisfaction. In many studies they are discussed as potential antecedents—things in the workplace that might drive satisfaction or lead to dissatisfaction. One thing to keep in mind is that most of the research about factors that might contribute to job satisfaction is based on survey methods that do not clearly indicate direction of effects. In most cases such studies show that environmental factors are related to job satisfaction, but it is not clear that they are driving satisfaction. That does not mean that people's satisfaction is divorced from job factors. It is just that we cannot be certain in all cases if factors discussed in this chapter are clearly contributing to satisfaction. Such conclusions are best based on intervention studies that show how changing a job factor might affect job satisfaction.

In this chapter, I will discuss factors in the job environment and the work itself that are associated with job satisfaction. This includes how people are treated, the nature of job tasks, relations with other people in the workplace, and rewards. Also important to understanding job satisfaction

DOI: 10.4324/9781003250616-4

are individual factors that the person brings to the job. This includes both personality and prior experiences which will be covered in the following chapter. Both categories of hypothesized antecedents have the potential to work together to influence employee job satisfaction. The fit between the individual and the job has been shown to be an important influence on employee job satisfaction (Kristof, 1996). This too will be covered in the following chapter.

Job Characteristics

It has long been believed that routine, simple jobs such as we find on the traditional assembly line are inherently boring and dissatisfying (Hulin & Blood, 1968). The most influential theory of how job characteristics affect people is Hackman and Oldham's job characteristics theory (Hackman & Oldham, 1976, 1980). The basis of this theory is that people can be motivated by the intrinsic satisfaction they find in doing job tasks that are enjoyable. When they find their work to be interesting and meaningful, people will like their jobs and be motivated to perform well. The theory is illustrated in Figure 4.1. It shows how five core characteristics of jobs induce three psychological states that, in turn, lead to job performance, job satisfaction, motivation, and turnover. The five core characteristics can be applied to any job. They are:

- Skill variety: Number of skills it takes to do a job.
- Task identity: Doing a complete job rather than a small part.
- Task significance: Impact a job has on others or society.
- Autonomy: Control over how, when, and where to do tasks.
- Job feedback: Extent to which it is obvious when a task is done correctly.

The five core characteristics are proposed to lead to three psychological states. Skill variety, task identity, and task significance combined induce experienced meaningfulness of work. Autonomy leads to feelings of responsibility. Feedback results in knowledge of results about the products of work. The three psychological states, in turn, contribute to important outcomes of job satisfaction and motivation of employees.

According to job characteristics theory, the five core characteristics determine how motivating a job is likely to be. The Motivation Potential Score or MPS for a job is a combination of the five core characteristics that reflects job

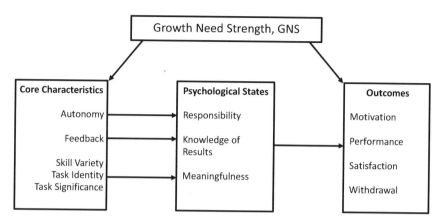

Figure 4.1 Illustration of the Hackman and Oldham (1976) Job Characteristics Model.

complexity or scope. The MPS is determined by mathematically combining scores on the five core characteristics using the following formula:

$$MPS = (SV + TI + TS)/3 \times Autonomy \times Feedback,$$

where SV = Skill Variety, TI = Task Identity, and TS = Task Significance.

The first three core characteristics are averaged, and that average is multiplied by the other two. The theory predicts that the higher the MPS score of a job, in other words, the higher its scope, the more motivating and satisfying it will be. The multiplicative nature of this formula implies that a job must induce all three psychological states to be motivating. If one of the three multiplicative terms in the equation is equal to zero, the job will not be at all motivating or satisfying.

Hackman and Oldham (1976) included a personality variable in their theory. Growth need strength or GNS was hypothesized to be a moderator of the effects of the core characteristics. A moderator is a variable that influences the relationship between other variables. For example, if the relationship between autonomy and job satisfaction was different between men and women, gender would be a moderator variable that affects the relationship between the two other variables.

The GNS variable reflects an individual's need for fulfillment of higher order needs, such as autonomy or personal growth. The theory states that the motivating effects of job characteristics will occur only for individuals

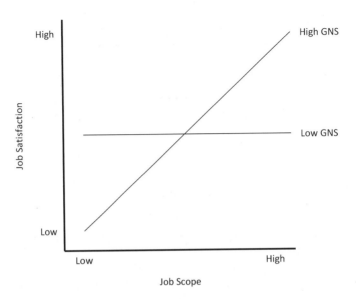

Figure 4.2 The moderating effect of growth need strength on the job scope-job satisfaction relationship.

who are high in GNS. Although they did not discuss people who were low, it is assumed that they did not expect such individuals to be motivated by jobs that were high on MPS. Figure 4.2 illustrates how the relationship between MPS and job satisfaction is moderated by GNS.

Simply put, the job characteristics theory states that people who prefer challenge and interest in their work will be happier and more motivated if they have high-scope jobs, as defined by the five core characteristics. Such people would be likely to avoid very simple jobs, however, and might be attracted to managerial or professional work that provides higher levels of complexity.

Hackman and Oldham (1975) developed the Job Diagnostic Survey or JDS to assess the variables in their theory. This scale has been the most popular measure of job characteristics among academic researchers in this field. The JDS also included the measure of job satisfaction that I covered in Chapter 2. Other measures of job characteristics also have been developed. The most popular alternative measure is the Job Characteristics Index or JCI (Sims, Szilagyi, & Keller, 1976), which assesses four of the five JDS characteristics (Autonomy, Feedback, Skill variety, and Task identity). The JCI tends to have better reliability than the JDS, primarily due to its greater number of items per subscale (Fried, 1991). Note that links to the JCI and JDS can be found in my assessment archive (see Table A.2).

Most job characteristics studies have used measures such as the JCI or JDS completed by job incumbents to assess the job. These studies have found that incumbent reports of job characteristics significantly correlate with job satisfaction and motivation. Meta-analyses that mathematically combine results across studies provide estimates of how strongly these measures are related. Wegman, Hoffman, Carter, Twenge, and Guenole (2018) summarized results of studies using the JDS, finding that the five core task characteristics correlated from 0.26 (Task Identity) to 0.39 (Autonomy). Meta-analyses have also supported the hypothesized role of growth need strength (Loher, Noe, Moeller, & Fitzgerald, 1985; Spector, 1985). Studies have found larger correlations between job characteristics and job satisfaction for people who are higher than people who are lower on this personality variable.

There have been many critics of survey-based research to test the hypotheses of job characteristics theory (Frese & Zapf, 1988; Spector, 1992; Taber & Taylor, 1990). Much of the criticism has concerned what the incumbent measures such as the JDS reflect. Both Spector (1992) and Taber and Taylor (1990) discussed evidence that incumbent measures may be affected by many things besides objective features of the job. For example, people who are satisfied with their jobs are likely to perceive them as higher in scope than their counterparts who dislike their jobs, because they have a global positive impression of the job that colors their perceptions. Another problem is that most studies in this area merely demonstrate that job characteristics are correlated with job satisfaction. Those studies do not shed much light on job characteristics as an antecedent of job satisfaction. It is possible that many findings are due to the opposite possibility that job satisfaction affects people's perceptions of job characteristics. Although many of the findings we have discussed are suggestive that job characteristics contribute to job satisfaction, other types of studies are needed to test this hypothesis.

Although research with incumbent reports show a clear link with job satisfaction, we must look to other types of studies for evidence that job characteristics affect job satisfaction. Experiments have been conducted in both laboratory and field settings to see if manipulations of job characteristics would affect job satisfaction and other hypothesized outcomes. Some of these studies have found that these outcomes were affected as hypothesized by job scope (e.g., Ganster, 1980; Griffin, 1991; Kim, 1980; Wall, Corbett, Martin, Clegg, & Jackson, 1990), whereas others have found nonsignificant or weak effects (Griffeth, 1985; Lawler III, Hackman, & Kaufman, 1973).

Several researchers have used nonincumbent measures of job characteristics, such as observer- or supervisor-ratings of jobs, in addition to employee-reports. Results of these studies have found inconsistent correlations of job characteristics with job satisfaction. For example, Spector and Jex (1991) compared incumbent JDS ratings with job characteristics data generated by job analysts who never met the incumbents. Although the incumbent measures of job characteristics correlated significantly with job satisfaction, the analyst measures did not. Glick, Jenkins, and Gupta (1986) found that incumbent measures of job characteristics correlated much more strongly with job satisfaction (multiple R −0.43) than did observer ratings of job characteristics (multiple R = 0.15).

One reason for inconsistencies of results may have been the focus on JDS dimensions in most studies. Melamed, Ben-Avi, Luz, and Green (1995) operationalized job characteristics as task cycle time for a factory worker, which is the amount of time it takes to complete a task on the job. Cycle time is relevant to monotony, as repetitive jobs have tasks with the shortest cycle times. They found that the longer the cycle time for a job, the greater the job satisfaction.

Some of the strongest evidence that changing job characteristics can affect job satisfaction comes from Griffin (1991), but that change might not be maintained over time. Griffin conducted a longitudinal study of a job redesign in a bank with measurements taken before, immediately following, and two years after the redesign. Job satisfaction increased immediately following the job change, showing that increasing the scope of a job can result in greater job satisfaction. However, it returned to the pre-change level by the end of a two-year follow-up. Interestingly, scores on the JDS also increased right after the redesign, but they were maintained at the two-year follow-up assessment. These results suggest that the self-reports on the JDS reflected the levels of the job characteristics over the timeframe of the study, but the impact of the job characteristics on job satisfaction was transitory. This result is consistent with an expectancy or Hawthorne effect. Job satisfaction may have improved just because management was paying attention to the well-being of employees, or perhaps because of the novelty of the change that produced some excitement. The nature of the change may have had little to do with the outcome. In fact evidence exists that anticipation of change can have more of an effect on job satisfaction than the change itself (Salancik & Pfeffer, 1978). For example, a management announcement of an upcoming improvement at work can itself be seen as something very positive by employees, who then would report enhanced job satisfaction for at least a short time.

It seems likely from the existing research that job characteristics affect job satisfaction. However, it also seems likely that not everyone responds favorably to jobs that are high in job scope. The design of jobs that maximizes employee job satisfaction is difficult and must consider the personalities of employees. Employee job satisfaction is likely to be positively related to job characteristics when employees have choice in how their jobs are structured. In other words, job satisfaction is likely to be high when people have the job characteristics that they prefer.

Job Stress

On every job there will be conditions and situations that employees find stressful. Being yelled at by an irate customer or having a machine break while rushing to meet a deadline are stressful events that can be common for some jobs. Warr and Payne (1983) conducted a survey of working adults in Britain in which they asked if they had been emotionally upset by something that happened the prior day at work. Of those surveyed, 15% of men and 10% of women indicated having been upset by work. These sorts of situations can affect not only transitory emotional states, but more long-term job satisfaction as well.

There are two important categories of variables in job stress research. A job stressor is a condition or event at work that requires an adaptive response by a person (Beehr & Newman, 1978), such as being yelled at or having to complete a difficult assignment by a particular deadline. A job strain is the response to a job stressor, such as the emotion of anxiety or the physical symptom of a headache. Jex and Beehr (1991) categorized strains into behavioral reactions (e.g., leaving work early), physical reactions (e.g., hypertension), and psychological reactions (e.g., frustration). Job dissatisfaction has been one of the most frequently studied psychological strain reactions. In this section, we will discuss how several of the more frequently studied stressors relate to job satisfaction.

Organizational Constraints

Conditions of the job environment that interfere with employee job performance are called organizational constraints. The constraints come from many aspects of the job, including other people and the physical work environment. Peters, O'Connor, and Rudolf (1980) used the critical incident technique to develop a taxonomy of constraint areas. They surveyed 62 working people about their experience with organizational constraints on the job. Each subject described a constraint incident that interfered with their job performance. A content analysis of the responses was used to derive the eight areas shown in Table 4.1.

Although the major focus of organizational constraints research has been on job performance (Peters & O'Connor, 1980), it has been shown to relate to job satisfaction, as well. Employees who perceive high levels of constraints tend to be globally dissatisfied with their jobs (see meta-analysis by Pindek & Spector, 2016). O'Connor, Peters, Rudolf, and Pooyan (1982) reported correlations of organizational constraints with five job satisfaction facets:

- Coworker = −0.30
- Pay = −0.26
- Promotion = −0.28
- Supervision = −0.42
- Work itself = −0.31

The largest correlation with supervision satisfaction likely reflects that supervisors are the biggest source of constraints as seen by subordinates.

Table 4.1 The Eight Peters and O'Connor (1980) Organizational Constraint Areas

Area	Description
Job-related information	Information needed for the job.
Tools and equipment	Tools and equipment necessary for the job.
Materials and supplies	Materials and supplies necessary for the job.
Budgetary support	Money necessary to acquire resources to do the job.
Required services and help	Help available from other people.
Task preparation	Whether or not the employee has the knowledge, skill, ability and other characteristics necessary for the job.
Time availability	The amount of time available for doing the job.
Work environment	The physical features of the job environment.

Although these results might be interpreted as reflecting the effects of the job environment on employees, the reliance on incumbent self-report methods makes this conclusion tentative. Stronger evidence is found in a study by Fox, Spector, Goh, and Bruursema (2007) showing that an employee's job satisfaction was related to a coworker's report of that employee's constraints.

Role Stressors

One approach to viewing the interaction of employees and jobs is from the perspective of roles (Katz & Kahn, 1978). A role is the required pattern of behavior for an individual in the organization. Organizational roles can be associated with job positions or titles, but they are not identical as each person can have several roles, and not everyone with the same job title necessarily has the same role. For example, one person in an office might have the role of managing the coffee pot and supplies, even though it is not a formal part of the job. Often the person develops the role by taking on a task that others then assume will become that person's responsibility.

There are three aspects of roles that can be stressful and each of these role stressors is linked to job satisfaction, as shown in a meta-analysis by Eatough, Chang, Miloslavic, and Johnson (2011). In each case, high levels of the job stressor are associated with low job satisfaction.

- **Role ambiguity** is the degree of certainty the employee has about what their functions and responsibilities are. In many jobs the expectations of supervisors concerning the subordinate's roles are not clearly delineated, leading to employees experiencing role ambiguity. Of the three role stressors, it has the strongest relationship with job satisfaction with a mean correlation of −0.46 (Eatough et al., 2011).
- **Role conflict** exists when people experience incompatible demands about their functions and responsibilities. Intra-role conflict occurs when the conflict involves different people at work or different functions. This happens, for example, when two supervisors make demands that conflict or when the individual must accomplish two things, but only has time to accomplish one of them. For example, one supervisor might ask an employee to run an errand while another asks the employee to take a phone call. Extra-role conflict occurs when there are

conflicts between work and nonwork. The most frequently discussed form of extra-role conflict occurs between family and work responsibilities that will be discussed in a later section. The Eatough et al. (2011) meta-analysis found a mean correlation of role conflict with job satisfaction of −0.42.

• **Role Overload** is the extent to which a person has more work than they can do well. Overload can put a person under pressure which can lead to feelings of being overwhelmed at work. It has the smallest relationship among the role stressors with job satisfaction with a mean r of −0.32 (Eatough et al., 2011).

As with job characteristics, the survey results show that role stressors are related to job satisfaction, but they do not provide conclusive evidence that they drive dissatisfaction. There have been very few studies that have used more conclusive methodologies. One attempt was a laboratory study by J. K. Hall (1990) who experimentally manipulated role ambiguity for college students who completed an in-basket exercise. Her exercise was a paper and pencil problem solving task that is commonly found in assessment centers to select managers. Hall found no effect of role ambiguity on job satisfaction. Of course, student reactions in the laboratory might be different from those of employees at work.

Workload

Workload is defined as the level of task demands placed on the employee by the job. Qualitative workload is the effort required by job tasks or the level of difficulty both mental and physical. Having to lift heavy objects and having to solve difficult mathematics problems both reflect qualitative workload. By contrast, quantitative workload is the amount of work that the employee must do. Is there a little to accomplish each day, or a lot? This is distinguished from work overload, which refers to feeling that there is too much work to do. Although workload and overload should be related, it is possible for one person to feel overloaded with a relatively moderate level of workload, whereas another person might not feel overloaded even though the workload is heavy.

Workload has been found to correlate with job dissatisfaction as well as other job strains, such as burnout and physical health symptoms (Bowling,

Alarcon, Bragg, & Hartman, 2015). In their meta-analysis, Bowling et al. (2015) found a mean correlation of workload with global job satisfaction that was about half the size of the mean correlation for work overload found by Eatough et al. (2011).

Control

Control is the freedom that employees are given to make decisions about their work. Autonomy, which we discussed earlier as part of the job characteristics theory, is a form of control limited to the employee's own job tasks. Control is a broader term that includes aspects of the organization that have little to do directly with an employee's own tasks. Often individuals are allowed to have input into broad policy issues that afford them an expanded sense of control in the organization. Such control can have positive effects on a person's job satisfaction.

Control is an important variable in the job stress process. It has been found to correlate significantly with all three categories of job strains, especially psychological ones (Jex & Beehr, 1991). Spector (1986) conducted a meta-analysis relating measures of perceived control with job satisfaction. The results are summarized in Table 4.2, showing the mean correlations across studies of both global and facet job satisfaction. As can be seen in the table, correlations are largest for the intrinsic job satisfaction facets of growth and nature of work and smallest for extrinsic job satisfaction facets of coworkers and pay.

The control studies included in Spector's (1986) meta-analysis assessed perceived control. It is not clear that the correlations between control and job satisfaction in these studies reflect the effects of the objective

Table 4.2 Correlations of Job Satisfaction with Perceived Control from Spector's (1986) Meta-analysis

Facet	Number of Samples	Number of Subjects	Mean Correlation
Global	61	21,096	0.30
Coworkers	12	1,767	0.19
Nature of work	30	5,764	0.35
Pay	12	1,767	0.19
Promotion	13	2,094	0.20
Supervision	27	6,662	0.34
Nature of work	30	5,764	0.35

environment on people. As noted previously, reports about the job can be affected by how an employee feels about that job (Spector, 1992).

To get around this problem, we need studies that assess more objective measures of control. Studies of machine pacing provide insights into how objective control affects employees. For some tasks, the pace of work is determined by a machine rather than the employee. Machines often control the pace of factory work on assembly lines, but computers have been pacing the work of employees in an expanding number of jobs outside of manufacturing. Although the impact of machine pacing has not been well studied, the limited research hints that it might have detrimental effects on people (e.g., Frankenhaeuser & Johansson, 1986). Smith, Hurrell, and Murphy (1981) compared postal workers who were machine paced with those in similar jobs who were not. The machine paced employees had lower job satisfaction.

Mistreatment

Depending upon the job, employees can be subject to a wide range of physical and psychological mistreatment. These forms are discussed under a variety of terms that differ from a theoretical perspective. How they have been assessed has had a great deal of overlap so that it is difficult to clearly distinguish them across studies (Hershcovis, 2011). Such acts include:

- **Bullying** is a repeated pattern of physical and/or verbal acts that demean and hurt an individual over time. Such experiences can lead to poorer mental and physical health (Hansen, Hogh, & Persson, 2011). Individuals who report being bullied also report lower job satisfaction (Nielsen & Einarsen, 2012).
- **Incivility** is a mild form of mistreatment in which people experience insensitive or rude comments by others, often without it being clear that they had hostile intent (Pearson, Andersson, & Porath, 2005). As with other forms of mistreatment, it correlates negatively with job satisfaction (Yao, Lim, Guo, Ou, & Ng, 2021).
- **Interpersonal conflict** has to do with arguments and disputes among people that can arise over personality clashes or disagreements about the work. Conflict has been linked to job dissatisfaction (Bowling & Beehr, 2006).

- **Ostracism** occurs when employees are ignored and isolated by coworkers. This is a passive form of mistreatment that involves actively excluding a target from meetings and social gatherings, as well as ignoring the person and failing to respond to e-mails. Those who are ostracized at work have lower job satisfaction (see meta-analyses by Bedi, 2021; Howard, Cogswell, & Smith, 2020).
- **Physical violence** is when an employee is assaulted at work with or without a weapon. This is a common occurrence in some jobs that require close contact with the public, such as healthcare providers and police officers (Foley & Rauser, 2012). Exposure to violence is associated with job dissatisfaction (Kessler, Spector, Chang, & Parr, 2008).

Perceived Organizational Politics

In some workplaces, people will engage in self-serving political behaviors to the detriment of their coworkers (Bedi & Schat, 2013). These behaviors can be performed by individuals for their own gain or for the advantage of the groups to which they belong. In those cases, groups of individuals might band together to engage in political actions. Those actions can include manipulating and undermining others or finding ways to gain competitive advantages over others. For example, in a sales organization, some salespeople might manipulate customers to remain loyal to them by telling falsehoods about other salespeople and why they should not deal with them. Working in such an organization has been linked to job dissatisfaction (Bedi & Schat, 2013; Miller, Rutherford, & Kolodinsky, 2008).

Demand/Control Model

The Demand/Control Model (Karasek, 1979) hypothesizes that control and job stressors interact in their effects on job strains, including job dissatisfaction. Demands are stressors such as workload that have the potential to induce strain in people. Control acts as a buffer to reduce the effects of demands. When an employee has high control, demands will have little relationship with job strains. When the employee has little control, demands will be correlated with job strain. An important implication of this model is that the negative effects of demands can be reduced by increasing control.

Unfortunately, research support for the demand/control model has been inconsistent. Although main effects of control and demands on strains have been consistently shown, the buffering effect of control on the demand-strain relationship has been found in only some studies (de Lange, Taris, Kompier, Houtman, & Bongers, 2003). There are several issues that might explain the inconsistencies. First, different studies have used different measures of control and demands, so it might be that only some types of control are buffers, or some types of demands are buffered. Second, moderator analysis requires large samples to achieve adequate statistical power to detect significant effects, and many studies were underpowered due to small samples. Third, for buffering to occur, the person must have control over the specific demand. Control in general would not be expected to be effective if it is unable to influence the specific stressors that people encounter.

The demand/control model has been expanded to include a third factor of social support that consists of actions others take in helping someone cope with stress at work (Johnson & Hall, 1988). The demand/control/support model suggests that both control and support buffer the effects of demands on strain. Social support at work has been linked to low levels of strains including job dissatisfaction. For example, Schantz, Coxe, and Bruk-Lee (2021) studied stress in police officers finding that those who received support from coworkers and supervisors had higher job satisfaction. As with the demand/control model, studies have been inconsistent in finding a buffering effect of support (de Lange et al., 2003).

Work-Family Conflict

Work-family conflict exists when demands of the family and demands of the job interfere with one another. The problem can occur for anyone with a family, but it is especially troublesome for two-career couples with children, and single parents. Conflict is likely when children are sick and when school activities require parent involvement.

Work-family conflict can occur in both directions—work can interfere with family and family can interfere with work. Carlson, Kacmar, and

Williams (2000) identified three types of conflict that can work in either direction.

- **Time-based conflict** occurs when an employee must be in two places at the same time (a meeting at work and a school event with a child) or doesn't have enough time to complete all family and work activities.
- **Strain-based conflict** occurs when the strain experienced in one domain spills over to the other. This can occur when an employee experiences stressors at work that lead to strains that the person takes home after work, such as coming home in a bad mood because of a stressful work event. The three role stressors we discussed earlier, for example, have been linked to work-family conflict (Ford, Heinen, & Langkamer, 2007).
- **Behavior-based conflict** occurs when a person has trouble "switching gears" from home to work or from work to home, engaging in behaviors in both domains that are only appropriate for one of them.

Job satisfaction has been found to correlate significantly with overall work-family conflict, and this relationship holds for both men and women (Hwang & Ramadoss, 2017). Employees who experience high levels of conflict tend to report low levels of job satisfaction, and this relationship is larger for work-family than family-work conflict (Michel, Mitchelson, Kotrba, LeBreton, & Baltes, 2009).

Work-family conflict is sometimes considered a women's issue, leading to the suggestion that there would be gender differences. A meta-analysis of more than 350 studies and over a quarter of a million employees finds few differences between men and women in their experience of work-family conflict (Shockley, Shen, DeNunzio, Arvan, & Knudsen, 2017). Further, the relationship between job satisfaction and work-family conflict holds equally for men and women (Hwang & Ramadoss, 2017). Clearly, work-family conflict can be an issue for all employees.

The negative effects of work-family conflict are not limited to the impact on employees. Stewart and Barling (1996) conducted a study to explore the impact of work-family conflict and job satisfaction on parenting behavior in a sample of employed fathers. Work-family conflict correlated -0.39 with job satisfaction, which, in turn, correlated significantly with parental practices. They used complex statistical procedures (structural equation modeling) to test a model they developed showing how conflict affects the children of employed parents. They found evidence that conflict contributes to job satisfaction, which leads to parental practice, which affects children's performance in school. This study demonstrates that there can be important ramifications of work conditions and job satisfaction that extend beyond the workplace.

Organizations can adopt family-friendly policies that either help people cope with or reduce work-family conflict. These policies including onsite childcare and flexible work schedules have been linked to reduced work-family conflict (Butts, Casper, & Yang, 2013). Behavior by supervisors that support employees with family responsibilities were also found to have positive effects (Butts et al., 2013). Even without formal policies, supervisors in many organizations have discretion to allow flexibility that reduces at least some work-family conflict.

Pay

The correlation between level of pay and job satisfaction tends to be surprisingly small. As might be expected, level of pay correlates more strongly with pay satisfaction (mean $r = 0.22$) than global job satisfaction (mean $r = -14$), although neither correlation is particularly large (see meta-analysis by Judge, Piccolo, Podsakoff, Shaw, & Rich, 2010). Although pay level is not an important issue, pay fairness can be very important. Most employees are not concerned that people in other occupations make more than they do. They are often quite concerned that people in the same occupation earn more. Rice, Phillips, and McFarlin (1990) reported a moderately large correlation of 0.50 between pay level and job satisfaction in a sample of mental health professionals who all had the same job. In a homogeneous sample people are likely to compare themselves to one another and be quite dissatisfied if their salary is lower than others in the same job. What can be even more important than salary differences, however, is procedural justice in pay policies. This means that people should perceive the policies and procedures by which salary is administered to be fair, even if it results in differential pay. This leads to the next topic of workplace justice.

Justice

People's perceptions of fairness and justice in how they and others are treated are important for employee attitudes and behaviors. Justice can be viewed from several perspectives, but the two that have received the most scrutiny are distributive justice and procedural justice. Distributive justice means that rewards are given in a systematic way according to contributions, whereas procedural justice has to do with the procedures used to allocate rewards (Ambrose & Arnaud, 2005). For example, if at the end of the year a supervisor has a pot of money to hand out as bonuses to their employees, distributive justice has to do with how much each person receives (e.g., percentage of basic salary), whereas procedural justice has to do with how the allocation approach was decided (e.g., vote of the group).

Both forms of justice have been linked to job satisfaction (Karam et al., 2019). In their meta-analysis, Cohen-Charash and Spector (2001) found that distributive and procedural justice related similarly to both global job satisfaction (mean weighted $r = 0.47$ and 0.43, respectively) and satisfaction with supervisor (mean weighted $r = 0.58$ and 0.57, respectively). For pay satisfaction, however, distributive justice had a significantly higher correlation than did procedural justice (mean weighted $r = 0.62$ vs. 0.48). This suggests that when it comes to pay satisfaction, employees are more sensitive to what they get than how they got it.

Work Schedules

The standard work shift for most people is approximately eight daylight hours per day for five weekdays each week. Nonstandard work schedules have become increasingly common, requiring longer shifts and working different days and times. Increasingly, organizations are operating more than eight hours per day, requiring extended hours for employees. At the same time many employers are offering flexibility in scheduling to accommodate individuals with families and other nonwork obligations. Of interest here will be four types of nonstandard work schedules: Flexible work schedules, long work shifts, night shifts, and part-time work.

Flexible Work Schedules

Although fixed work schedules are still found in most organizations, increasingly employees are being offered more flexible arrangements. There are many varieties of flexible schedules ranging from those allowing complete freedom to work at any time to those that allow discretion only in limited ways, such as being able to begin the workday one or two hours late and quitting after the required daily hours have been completed. The advantage to flexible schedules for the employer is that employees are encouraged to take care of personal business on their own time. Support for this notion is provided by studies which found that absence (Krausz & Freibach, 1983; Pierce & Newstrom, 1982) and tardiness (Ralston, 1989) are less with flexible work schedules.

In their meta-analysis Baltes, Briggs, Huff, Wright, and Neuman (1999) found that having flextime was associated with greater satisfaction with the work schedule. On the other hand, the correlation with global job satisfaction, although statistically significant, was quite small. However, the effect of flexibility on job satisfaction might have a lot to do with whether employees want flexibility. Kaduk, Genadek, Kelly, and Moen (2019) found that the relationship between voluntary flexibility and job satisfaction was positive, but the relationship between imposed flexibility and job satisfaction was negative.

Long Shifts

Long shifts are those that exceed the standard of eight hours per day. Many organizations use shifts of 10 and 12 hours, which have both advantages and disadvantages. The 10-hour shift allows for a 40-hour work week to be compressed into four days. A 12-hour shift provides coverage of the entire 24-hour day with two full shifts rather than three required with 8-hour shifts. It has become commonly used in hospitals and other organizations that require 24-hour staffing.

The most frequently noted problem with long shifts is fatigue (Ronen & Primps, 1981). However, employees also like longer shifts because they can provide more days off (Breaugh, 1983). The availability of more useable free time can sometimes overcome fatigue, which is in large part a psychological reaction. Pierce and Dunham (1992) surveyed police officers who worked either 8- or 12-hour shifts. The 12-hour officers reported less fatigue, which might have been due to reduced feelings of stress resulting from having three full days to recover from the demands of working.

The effects of long shifts on job satisfaction are usually positive. Although employees might experience more fatigue, they usually prefer long shifts and will enjoy increased job satisfaction if allowed to work fewer but longer days (see meta-analysis by Baltes et al., 1999).

A study that underscores the potentially adverse effects of working long hours was reported by Raggatt (1991). He investigated the effects of shift length on a sample of Australian bus drivers. Each driver drove a unique route that varied considerably in length, thus producing variation in shift length. A survey asked the drivers about job satisfaction, maladaptive behaviors (e.g., medication overuse), physical health problems, and psychological stress outcomes. Working excessive hours were associated with:

- Alcohol consumption
- Job dissatisfaction
- Passenger complaints
- Pill taking
- Sleep disturbance

Job dissatisfaction was associated with all these variables, as well as:

- Accidents
- Doctor visits
- Frequent speeding
- Health complaints
- Psychological symptoms of stress

A model was developed that presented a multi-stage process whereby having to work long hours leads to maladaptive behavior (e.g., alcohol and pill use) as well as sleep disturbance, which leads to job dissatisfaction and other job strains. Clearly for some jobs, excessively long shifts are not a good idea.

Night Shifts

Many organizations, such as hospitals and police departments, operate 24 hours per day requiring two or three shifts of workers to cover the entire day. Many employers use rotating shifts so that everyone takes turns working days, evening, and nights. Both working at night and rotating shifts have been found to have detrimental effects on at least some employees.

The biggest problem with night work is that the typical cycle of sleep/waking is disturbed. Circadian rhythms of physiological events occur regularly throughout the day. These include changes in body temperature and in blood stream hormone levels. Disruption of these cycles by working when the individual would normally be sleeping can lead to health problems.

The most frequent health problem associated with night shift work is sleep disturbance. People who work at night are more likely to have problems with sleeping than their day shift counterparts (Barton & Folkard, 1991). Koller, Kundi, and Cervinka (1978) also found that night shift workers were more likely to have digestive problems than day workers. This may be due at least in part to the secretion of digestive hormones which is lower at night than during the day (Akerstedt & Theorell, 1976).

Both Barton and Folkard (1991) and Jamal and Baba (1992) found that the adverse effects of night shift work might be due more to shift rotation than to night work itself. In both studies people on permanent night shifts were compared to people who were working nights periodically because of shift rotation. Barton and Folkard found that the adverse effects of night work on sleep did not occur for employees on permanent night shifts. Of more interest to our present discussion is the relation of shift work to job satisfaction in Jamal and Baba's study. Employees who were assigned to temporary night shifts had lower job satisfaction than individuals who worked permanent night shifts. Thus, working nights itself does not seem to affect job satisfaction, but rotating from day shift to night shift might have a detrimental effect on employee feelings about the job.

Part-Time Work

Increasingly, organizations are hiring people to work fewer than the standard 40-hour week. Some of the motivation for this practice, at least in the U.S., is that part-timers do not have to be given the same fringe benefits, such as medical insurance, which adds substantial costs over and above pay. Since part-time employees do not get the same rewards, even when they do the same work, one might hypothesize that their job satisfaction would be lower than the job satisfaction of full-time employees. Interestingly, this does not seem to be the case.

Thorsteinson (2003) conducted a meta-analysis of 28 studies comparing part-time with full-time workers. There was no difference in global satisfaction between the two groups of workers. Feldman (1990) noted that the underlying causes of job satisfaction might be different for full-time and part-time employees. For example, many part-time employees are students who consider the job to be temporary. Schedule flexibility to minimize conflict with class schedules might be more important than benefits and rewards.

Virtual Work

As electronic communication has advanced, more and more employees have been able to work at least some of the time remotely from home or other locations. This trend toward virtual work (also called telework) or working from home rather than going to an employer's work location has become an important feature of the modern workplace. Although communicating in written form through e-mail and spoken form through telephone is far from new, the addition of video teleconferencing with platforms like MS Teams and Zoom has made virtual meetings widespread. The COVID-19 pandemic necessitated the use of these tools, and within a matter of months millions of employees became expert in navigating these systems and were using them as a major means of communication.

Virtual tools provide advantages for employees by allowing greater flexibility and more efficient use of time. On the other hand there can be disadvantages as employees feel isolated, have trouble communicating with others and developing trust, and experience low motivation (Dulebohn & Hoch, 2017). Studies comparing people who work virtually versus in an office have had mixed results, with some studies finding greater satisfaction for virtual workers (Fonner & Roloff, 2010), some finding lower satisfaction (Golden & Veiga, 2008), and some finding no difference (Morganson, Major, Oborn, Verive, & Heelan, 2010). There are two factors that might affect whether virtual workers are more satisfied with work. First, there is the extent to which virtual work is voluntary, as having control over virtual work can be helpful. In the Fonner and Roloff (2010) study, their teleworkers self-selected to work from home. A second has to do with the quality of supervision and relationships between the employee and supervisor. Golden and Veiga (2008) found an overall negative relationship between virtual work and job satisfaction, but the effect was moderated by quality of relationship with the supervisor reflected in their leader-member exchange or LMX. As shown in Figure 4.3 the quality of relationship with the supervisor determined whether the effect of telework on job satisfaction was positive or negative. For those with good supervisory relationships, satisfaction was higher with telework. With those with poor supervisory relationships, satisfaction was lower with telework. This means that the most satisfied employees were those who teleworked and had good relationships with supervisors. The least satisfied were those who teleworked and had poor relationships with supervisors. For employees who worked from the employer's location, satisfaction fell between the other two groups. Another way to look at this finding is that leadership quality becomes more important when employee telework.

Leadership

One of the most important determinants of employees' job experiences concerns the behavior of their supervisors. There are two ways to view leadership. First, there is the quality of relationship between leaders and

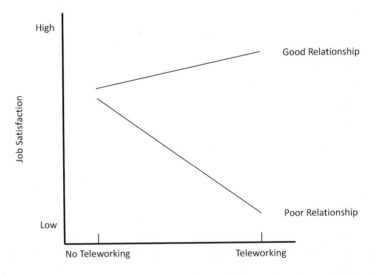

Figure 4.3 The moderating effect of relationship quality on the relationship between teleworking and job satisfaction.

followers reflected in leader-member exchange or LMX as I mentioned in the prior section (Graen & Uhl-Bien, 1995). That is, how well do leaders get along with each follower; do they have a good working relationship based on mutual respect, or is the relationship strained? Meta-analyses clearly show that the quality of relationships reflected in high LMX is associated with good global job satisfaction (Banks et al., 2014; Rockstuhl, Dulebohn, Ang, & Shore, 2012).

The second view has to do with overall leadership style reflecting the sorts of leader behaviors in which the leader typically engages. There have been several different kinds of behaviors that have been studied that relate to employee job satisfaction.

- **Consideration and Initiating Structure.** These two dimensions of leadership came from the classic Ohio State Leadership Studies (Fleishman & Harris, 1962). Consideration is showing concern for the well-being of employees. Initiating structure has to do with organizing and managing employee tasks. Both dimensions are related positively with job satisfaction with consideration having the larger relationship (see meta-analysis by Judge, Piccolo, & Ilies, 2004).
- **Moral Forms of Leadership**. Several styles of leadership have been identified that are based on ethical and moral principles. Such leaders hold high standards of conduct for themselves and followers. Lemoine, Hartnell, and Leroy (2019) distinguished the three main types of moral leadership as:
  - Authentic leaders are aware of their own morals and values and encourage followers to engage in high moral standards. The focus is on displaying true feelings.
  - Ethical leaders emphasize high ethical standards for themselves and others.
  - Servant leaders view their role as serving others and put the well-being of followers as high priority.

  All three forms of moral leadership are associated with job satisfaction (Hoch, Bommer, Dulebohn, & Wu, 2018).

- **Transformational and Transactional Leadership**. Bass, Avolio, and Atwater (1996) distinguished two types of leadership: Transformational and transactional. A transformational leader is one who inspires and motivates employees by providing a vision and supporting employees in their personal development. A transactional leader adopts an exchange or tit-for-tat approach of offering rewards for accomplishing what the leader wants. Both forms are associated with job satisfaction (Aydin, Sarier, & Uysal, 2013; Ng, 2017).

Organizational Climate

Organizational climate concerns the policies and practices of an organization to encourage behaviors that help achieve organizational objectives and discourage behaviors that interfere with those objectives (Zohar, 2010). Most research on climate has concerned types of behaviors designed to achieve goals within a category, such as innovation or employee safety.

A climate is a property of an organization or a unit of an organization such as a department or work team. It follows that the perceptions of climate by individuals within a unit or even the whole organization should agree, at least to some extent. If people do not agree, then climate is merely the idiosyncratic perception of individuals, which might reflect that each person's experience is unique, or that experiences are shared but viewed differently. As it winds up, organizations differ in the extent to which people agree about the climate, a concept called climate strength (Luria, 2008). Some organizations do a good job of building a climate that employees can agree about whereas others do not communicate clearly about what is important.

Climate is typically assessed with questionnaires administered to employees. It can be studied at the level of individual employees as *perceived climate*, linking it to other variables such as job satisfaction. Climate can be studied at the organizational unit level, such as departments or workgroups, as *organizational climate*. In such studies the individual perceptions are aggregated by taking the average within each unit. This aggregate-level climate can then be related to aggregate-level outcomes, such as number (or rate) of injuries within each factory or total sales within each sales team. The distinction between individual level and unit level is important, as there is no guarantee that relationships will be the same at both levels. It is possible that individuals who are high on a particular climate will have higher job satisfaction, whereas mean perceptions do not predict mean satisfaction for individual workgroups. The assumption that relationships that hold at one level will necessarily hold at another is the ecological fallacy

(Brewer & Venaik, 2014). It is quite possible that the correlates of perceived climate at the individual level will be different than correlations of organizational climate at the workgroup level for statistical reasons beyond the scope of this book.

There are many climate types that have been identified and studied, and many have been linked to job satisfaction. High levels of perceived, and/or organizational climate are associated with high levels or job satisfaction, as well as other outcomes. Some of the more popular climates that have been linked to job satisfaction are:

- **Customer Service Climate**: This climate reflects the emphasis on putting the customer first and providing top-notch service. As might be expected, good customer service climates are linked to good service performance (e.g., Way, Sturman, & Raab, 2010). They are also linked to high levels of job satisfaction at both the employee (Menguc, Auh, Katsikeas, & Jung, 2016) and unit (Shepherd, Ployhart, & Kautz, 2020) levels, perhaps because climates that result in more sales have better rewards that lead to job satisfaction. I will return to the connection between job satisfaction and sales in Chapter 6.
- **Diversity Climate**: An organization with a diversity climate is inclusive in its actions and values people's differences, including demographic diversity (e.g., age, gender, or race) and other kinds of diversity (e.g., abilities, backgrounds, neurodiversity, or values). Such climates are associated with high job satisfaction among employees (Madera, Dawson, & Neal, 2013; McCallaghan, Jackson, & Heyns, 2019).
- **Ethical Climate**: An organization with an ethical climate places emphasis on maintaining high ethical standards in dealing with clients, customers, patients, and other employees. Ethical climates have been linked to high job satisfaction at both the individual (Jang & Oh, 2019) and unit levels (Wang & Hsieh, 2012).
- **Psychosocial Safety Climate**: This climate emphasizes the psychological safety of employees by reducing the risk that they will be bullied or mistreated at work (Hall, Dollard, & Coward, 2010). Such climates are associated with low rates of mistreatment as might be expected (Dollard, Dormann, Tuckey, & Escartín, 2017). They are also associated with high job satisfaction (Hall, Dollard, Winefield, Dormann, & Bakker, 2013).

- **Safety Climate**: An organization with a safety climate focuses on keeping employees physically safe from accidents or injuries. This has been the most studied form of climate, so much so that several meta-analyses have been published about it. As might be expected, a good safety climate is associated with fewer injuries at work (see meta-analysis by Beus, Payne, Bergman, & Arthur, 2010). It has also been consistently associated in a meta-analysis with better overall well-being and job satisfaction (Clarke, 2010).
- **Violence Prevention Climate**: A type of safety climate that focuses specifically on being assaulted at work is violence prevention climate (Kessler et al., 2008). Not only are high levels of this climate associated with low rates of violence, but it is also linked to high job satisfaction (Yang, Caughlin, Gazica, Truxillo, & Spector, 2014). There have been several types of climates developed that relate to employee physical and psychological safety as I noted above. Hutchinson, Andel, and Spector (2018) argued that they all reflected a general tendency for organizations to emphasize employee safety and well-being as scales to assess different forms of safety were strongly related to one another, and related similarly to injuries, mistreatment, and violence at work, as well as job satisfaction.

There is a pattern in the studies of different kinds of climate that suggests organizations with a strong emphasis on outcomes that can be positive for employees, be it ethics, performance, or well-being have more satisfied employees. These climates reflect supportive environments with clear-cut expectations for employees that reduce the stress of uncertainty. Knowing that your employer is concerned with your well-being is certainly something that will be seen positively. But knowing that there is support for doing the job itself, for example, by emphasizing good customer service can also be seen positively by employees.

Factors External to the Organization

To this point we have discussed factors in the work and family environments and how they link to job satisfaction. Another set of potentially important factors occur outside of the organization and family. National crises arise that affect the workplace from the outside. This might include financial, health, and political crises that affect a single country or the entire world.

One such crisis is COVID-19 that had a significant impact on work for most employees. For those in healthcare and what were considered essential workers, the impact was on personal safety and the risk of being exposed to the disease at work. Many healthcare and other essential workers were infected. Employees not considered essential, such as university faculty and staff, were required to work from home, many for the first time. This required overnight adjustments to working virtually with little training and in many cases, inadequate equipment, or limited web access.

The impact of the COVID-19 pandemic can be seen in ongoing longitudinal studies of job satisfaction. One such study, conducted by Möhring et al. (2021), made use of the German Internet Panel (GIP) that consisted of people who were surveyed before the pandemic in September 2019 and during the COVID lockdown in April 2020. Results showed that job satisfaction declined during this time. Likewise, in another study in a single hospitality company job satisfaction declined from July 2019 to July 2020, as perceived job demands and emotional strain increased (Venkatesh, Ganster, Schuetz, & Sykes, 2021).

Economic crises might also affect how people feel about work. When economic conditions are poor, access to good jobs can be difficult. Companies might have to reduce the size of their workforces to survive, and employees can feel the weight of increased demands during a time when alternative employment can be difficult to find. Indeed, studies have linked poor economic conditions and high unemployment rates lead to low job satisfaction at the individual employee (Tay & Harter, 2013) and societal levels (Augner, 2015; Tay & Harter, 2013).

References

Akerstedt, T., & Theorell, T. (1976). Exposure to night work: Serum gastrin reactions, psychosomatic complaints and personality variables. *Journal of Psychosomatic Research, 20,* 479–484. doi: 10.1016/0022-3999(76)90012-x

Ambrose, M. L., & Arnaud, A. (2005). Are procedural justice and distributive justice distinct? In J. Greenberg & J. A. Colquitt (Eds.), *Handbook of organizational justice* (pp. 59–84). Mahwah, NJ: Lawrence Erlbaum.

Augner, C. (2015). Job satisfaction in the European Union: The role of macroeconomic, personal, and job-related factors. *Journal of Occupational and Environmental Medicine, 57,* 241–245. doi: 10.1097/JOM.0000000000000398

Aydin, A., Sarier, Y., & Uysal, Ş. (2013). The effect of school principals' leadership styles on teachers' organizational commitment and job satisfaction. *Kuram ve Uygulamada Eğitim Bilimleri, 13*, 806–811.

Baltes, B. B., Briggs, T. E., Huff, J. W., Wright, J. A., & Neuman, G. A. (1999). Flexible and compressed workweek schedules: A meta-analysis of their effects on work-related criteria. *Journal of Applied Psychology, 84*, 496–513. doi: 10.1037/0021-9010.84.4.496

Banks, G. C., Batchelor, J. H., Seers, A., O'Boyle, E. H., Jr., Pollack, J. M., & Gower, K. (2014). What does team-member exchange bring to the party? A meta-analytic review of team and leader social exchange. *Journal of Organizational Behavior, 35*, 273–295. doi: 10.1002/job.1885

Barton, J., & Folkard, S. (1991). The response of day and night nurses to their work schedules. *Journal of Occupational Psychology, 64*, 207–218. doi: 10.1111/j.2044-8325.1991.tb00555.x

Bass, B. M., Avolio, B. J., & Atwater, L. E. (1996). The transformational and transactional leadership of men and women. *Applied Psychology: An International Review, 45*, 5–34.

Bedi, A. (2021). No herd for black sheep: A meta-analytic review of the predictors and outcomes of workplace ostracism. *Applied Psychology: An International Review, 70*, 861–904. doi: 10.1111/apps.12238

Bedi, A., & Schat, A. C. H. (2013). Perceptions of organizational politics: A meta-analysis of its attitudinal, health, and behavioural consequences. *Canadian Psychology/Psychologie canadienne, 54*, 246–259. doi: 10.1037/a0034549

Beehr, T. A., & Newman, J. E. (1978). Job stress, employee health, and organizational effectiveness: A facet analysis, model, and literature review. *Personnel Psychology, 31*, 665–699.

Beus, J. M., Payne, S. C., Bergman, M. E., & Arthur, W., Jr. (2010). Safety climate and injuries: An examination of theoretical and empirical relationships. *Journal of Applied Psychology, 95*, 713–727. doi: 10.1037/a0019164

Bowling, N. A., Alarcon, G. M., Bragg, C. B., & Hartman, M. J. (2015). A meta-analytic examination of the potential correlates and consequences of workload. *Work & Stress, 29*, 95–113. doi: 10.1080/02678373.2015.1033037

Bowling, N. A., & Beehr, T. A. (2006). Workplace harassment from the victim's perspective: A theoretical model and meta-analysis. *Journal of Applied Psychology, 91*, 998–1012. doi: 10.1037/0021-9010.91.5.998

Breaugh, J. A. (1983). The 12-hour work day: Differing employee reactions. *Personnel Psychology, 36,* 277–288. doi: 10.1111/j.1744-6570.1983.tb01437.x

Brewer, P., & Venaik, S. (2014). The ecological fallacy in national culture research. *Organization Studies, 35,* 1063–1086. doi: 10.1177/0170840613517602

Butts, M. M., Casper, W. J., & Yang, T. S. (2013). How important are work-family support policies? A meta-analytic investigation of their effects on employee outcomes. *Journal of Applied Psychology, 98,* 1–25. doi: 10.1037/a0030389

Carlson, D. S., Kacmar, K., & Williams, L. J. (2000). Construction and initial validation of a multidimensional measure of work-family conflict. *Journal of Vocational Behavior, 56,* 249–276.

Clarke, S. (2010). An integrative model of safety climate: Linking psychological climate and work attitudes to individual safety outcomes using meta-analysis. *Journal of Occupational and Organizational Psychology, 83,* 553–578. doi: 10.1348/096317909X452122

Cohen-Charash, Y., & Spector, P. E. (2001). The role of justice in organizations: A meta-analysis. *Organizational Behavior and Human Decision Processes, 86,* 278–321. doi: 10.1006/obhd.2001.2958

de Lange, A. H., Taris, T. W., Kompier, M. A. J., Houtman, I. L. D., & Bongers, P. M. (2003). 'The very best of the millennium': Longitudinal research and the demand-control-(support) model. *Journal of Occupational Health Psychology, 8,* 282–305. doi: 10.1037/1076-8998.8.4.282

Dollard, M. F., Dormann, C., Tuckey, M. R., & Escartín, J. (2017). Psychosocial safety climate (PSC) and enacted PSC for workplace bullying and psychological health problem reduction. *European Journal of Work and Organizational Psychology, 26,* 844–857. doi: 10.1080/1359432X.2017.1380626

Dulebohn, J., & Hoch, J. (2017). Virtual teams in organizations. *Human Resource Management Review, 27,* 569–574. doi: 10.1016/j.hrmr.2016.12.004

Eatough, E. M., Chang, C.-H., Miloslavic, S. A., & Johnson, R. E. (2011). Relationships of role stressors with organizational citizenship behavior: A meta-analysis. *Journal of Applied Psychology, 96,* 619–632. doi: 10.1037/a0021887

Feldman, D. C. (1990). Reconceptualizing the nature and consequences of part-time work. *Academy of Management Review, 15,* 103–112. doi: 10.5465/amr.1990.4308279

Fleishman, E. A., & Harris, E. F. (1962). Patterns of leadership behavior related to employee grievances and turnover. *Personnel Psychology, 15,* 43–56.

Foley, M., & Rauser, E. (2012). Evaluating progress in reducing workplace violence: Trends in Washington State workers' compensation claims rates, 1997–2007. [Empirical Study; Quantitative Study]. *Work: Journal of Prevention, Assessment & Rehabilitation, 42,* 67–81.

Fonner, K. L., & Roloff, M. E. (2010). Why teleworkers are more satisfied with their jobs than are office-based workers: When less contact is beneficial. *Journal of Applied Communication Research, 38,* 336–361. doi: 10.1080/00909882.2010.513998

Ford, M. T., Heinen, B. A., & Langkamer, K. L. (2007). Work and family satisfaction and conflict: A meta-analysis of cross-domain relations. *Journal of Applied Psychology, 92,* 57–80. doi: 10.1037/0021-9010.92.1.57

Fox, S., Spector, P. E., Goh, A., & Bruursema, K. (2007). Does your coworker know what you're doing? Convergence of self- and peer-reports of counterproductive work behavior. *International Journal of Stress Management, 14,* 41–60. doi: 10.1037/1072-5245.14.1.41

Frankenhaeuser, M., & Johansson, G. (1986). Stress at work: Psychobiological and psychosocial aspects. *International Review of Applied Psychology, 35,* 287–299.

Frese, M., & Zapf, D. (1988). Methodological issues in the study of work stress: Objective vs subjective measurement of work stress and the question of longitudinal studies. In C. L. Cooper & R. Payne (Eds.), *Causes, coping and consequences of stress at work* (pp. 375–411). Oxford, England: John Wiley & Sons.

Fried, Y. (1991). Meta-analytic comparison of the Job Diagnostic Survey and Job Characteristics Inventory as correlates of work satisfaction and performance. *Journal of Applied Psychology, 76,* 690–697.

Ganster, D. C. (1980). Individual differences and task design: A laboratory experiment. *Organizational Behavior and Human Performance, 26,* 131–148. doi: https://doi.org/10.1016/0030-5073(80)90051-3

Glick, W. H., Jenkins, G., & Gupta, N. (1986). Method versus substance: How strong are underlying relationships between job characteristics and attitudinal outcomes? *Academy of Management Journal, 29,* 441–464.

Golden, T. D., & Veiga, J. F. (2008). The impact of superior--subordinate relationships on the commitment, job satisfaction, and performance of virtual workers. *The Leadership Quarterly, 19,* 77–88. doi: 10.1016/j.leaqua.2007.12.009

Graen, G. B., & Uhl-Bien, M. (1995). Relationship-based approach to leadership: Development of leader-member exchange (LMX) theory of leadership over 25 years: Applying a multi-level multi-domain perspective. *The Leadership Quarterly, 6*, 219–247. doi: 10.1016/1048-9843%2895%2990036-5

Griffeth, R. W. (1985). Moderation of the effects of job enrichment by participation: A longitudinal field experiment. *Organizational Behavior and Human Decision Processes, 35*, 73–93. doi: 10.1016/0749-5978(85)90045-7

Griffin, R. W. (1991). Effects of work redesign on employee perceptions, attitudes, and behaviors: A long-term investigation. *Academy of Management Journal, 34*, 425–435. doi: 10.2307/256449

Hackman, J. R., & Oldham, G. R. (1975). Development of the Job Diagnostic Survey. *Journal of Applied Psychology, 60*, 159–170.

Hackman, J. R., & Oldham, G. R. (1976). Motivation through design of work - Test of a theory. *Organizational Behavior and Human Performance, 16*, 250–279. doi: 10.1016/0030-5073(76)90016-7

Hackman, J. R., & Oldham, G. R. (1980). *Work redesign*. Reading, MA: Addison-Wesley.

Hall, G. B., Dollard, M. F., & Coward, J. (2010). Psychosocial safety climate: Development of the PSC-12. *International Journal of Stress Management, 17*, 353–383. doi: 10.1037/a0021320

Hall, G. B., Dollard, M. F., Winefield, A. H., Dormann, C., & Bakker, A. B. (2013). Psychosocial safety climate buffers effects of job demands on depression and positive organizational behaviors. *Anxiety, Stress & Coping: An International Journal, 26*, 355–377. doi: 10.1080/10615806.2012.700477

Hall, J. K. (1990). *Locus of control as a moderator of the relationship between perceived role ambiguity and reported work strains*. Unpublished Doctoral Dissertation. Tampa: University of South Florida

Hansen, A. M., Hogh, A., & Persson, R. (2011). Frequency of bullying at work, physiological response, and mental health. [Empirical Study; Quantitative Study]. *Journal of Psychosomatic Research, 70*, 19–27. doi: 10.1016/j.jpsychores.2010.05.010

Hershcovis, M. S. (2011). "Incivility, social undermining, bullying...oh my!": A call to reconcile constructs within workplace aggression research. *Journal of Organizational Behavior, 32*, 499–519. doi: 10.1002/job.689

Hoch, J. E., Bommer, W. H., Dulebohn, J. H., & Wu, D. (2018). Do ethical, authentic, and servant leadership explain variance above and beyond transformational leadership? A meta-analysis. *Journal of Management, 44,* 501–529. doi: 10.1177/0149206316665461

Howard, M. C., Cogswell, J. E., & Smith, M. B. (2020). The antecedents and outcomes of workplace ostracism: A meta-analysis. *Journal of Applied Psychology, 105,* 577–596. doi: 10.1037/apl0000453.supp (Supplemental)

Hulin, C. L., & Blood, M. R. (1968). Job enlargement, individual differences, and worker responses. *Psychological Bulletin, 69,* 41–55. doi: 10.1037/h0025356

Hutchinson, D. M., Andel, S. A., & Spector, P. E. (2018). Digging deeper into the shared variance among safety-related climates: the need for a general safety climate measure. *International Journal of Occupational and Environmental Health, 24,* 38–46. doi: 10.1080/10773525.2018.1507867

Hwang, W., & Ramadoss, K. (2017). The job demands-control-support model and job satisfaction across gender: The mediating role of work-family conflict. *Journal of Family Issues, 38,* 52–72. doi: 10.1177/0192513X16647983

Jamal, M., & Baba, V. V. (1992). Shiftwork and department-type related to job stress, work attitudes and behavioral intentions: A study of nurses. *Journal of Organizational Behavior, 13,* 449–464. doi: 10.1002/job.4030130503

Jang, Y., & Oh, Y. (2019). Impact of ethical factors on job satisfaction among Korean nurses. *Nursing Ethics, 26,* 1186–1198. doi: 10.1177/0969733017742959

Jex, S. M., & Beehr, T. A. (1991). Emerging theoretical and methodological issues in the study of work-related stress. *Research in Personnel and Human Resources Management, 9,* 311–365.

Johnson, J. V., & Hall, E. M. (1988). Job strain, work place social support, and cardiovascular-disease – A cross-sectional study of a random sample of the Swedish working population. *American Journal of Public Health, 78,* 1336–1342.

Judge, T. A., Piccolo, R. F., & Ilies, R. (2004). The Forgotten Ones? The Validity of Consideration and Initiating Structure in Leadership Research. *Journal of Applied Psychology, 89,* 36–51. doi: 10.1037/0021-9010.89.1.36

Judge, T. A., Piccolo, R. F., Podsakoff, N. P., Shaw, J. C., & Rich, B. L. (2010). The relationship between pay and job satisfaction: A meta-analysis of the literature. *Journal of Vocational Behavior, 77,* 157–167. doi: 10.1016/j.jvb.2010.04.002

Kaduk, A., Genadek, K., Kelly, E. L., & Moen, P. (2019). Involuntary vs voluntary flexible work: Insights for scholars and stakeholders. *Community, Work & Family, 22,* 412–442. doi: 10.1080/13668803.2019.1616532

Karam, E. P., Hu, J., Davison, R. B., Juravich, M., Nahrgang, J. D., Humphrey, S. E., & Scott DeRue, D. (2019). Illuminating the 'Face' of Justice: A meta-analytic examination of leadership and organizational justice. *Journal of Management Studies, 56*, 134–171. doi: 10.1111/joms.12402

Karasek, R. A., Jr. (1979). Job demands, job decision latitude, and mental strain: implications for job redesign. *Administrative Science Quarterly, 24*, 285–308. doi: 10.2307/2392498

Katz, D., & Kahn, R. L. (1978). *The social psychology of organizations* (2nd ed). New York City: John Wiley.

Kessler, S. R., Spector, P. E., Chang, C.-H., & Parr, A. D. (2008). Organizational violence and aggression: Development of the three-factor Violence Climate Survey. *Work & Stress, 22*, 108–124. doi: 10.1080/02678370802187926

Kim, J. S. (1980). Relationships of personality to perceptual and behavioral responses in stimulating and nonstimulating tasks. *Academy of Management Journal, 23*, 307–319. doi: 10.5465/255433

Koller, M., Kundi, M., & Cervinka, R. (1978). Field studies of shift work at an Austrian oil refinery I: Health and psychosocial wellbeing of workers who drop out of shiftwork. *Ergonomics, 21*, 835–847. doi: 10.1080/00140137808931787

Krausz, M., & Freibach, N. (1983). Effects of flexible working time for employed women upon satisfaction, strains, and absenteeism. *Journal of Occupational Psychology, 56*, 155–159. doi: 10.1111/j.2044-8325.1983.tb00123.x

Kristof, A. L. (1996). Person-organization fit: An integrative review of its conceptualizations, measurement, and implications. *Personnel Psychology, 49*, 1–49. doi: 10.1111/j.1744-6570.1996.tb01790.x

Lawler III, E. E., Hackman, J. R., & Kaufman, S. (1973). Effects of job redesign: A field experiment. *Journal of Applied Social Psychology, 3*, 49–62. doi: 10.1111/j.1559-1816.1973.tb01294.x

Lemoine, G. J., Hartnell, C., & Leroy, H. (2019). Taking stock of moral approaches to leadership: An integrative review of ethical, authentic, and servant leadership. *The Academy of Management Annals, 13*, 148–187. doi: 10.5465/annals.2016.0121

Loher, B. T., Noe, R. A., Moeller, N. L., & Fitzgerald, M. P. (1985). A meta-analysis of the relation of job characteristics to job satisfaction. *Journal of Applied Psychology, 70*, 280–289. doi: 10.1037/0021-9010.70.2.280

Luria, G. (2008). Climate strength – How leaders form consensus. *The Leadership Quarterly, 19*, 42–53. doi: 10.1016/j.leaqua.2007.12.004

Madera, J. M., Dawson, M., & Neal, J. A. (2013). Hotel managers' perceived diversity climate and job satisfaction: The mediating effects of role ambiguity and conflict. *International Journal of Hospitality Management, 35*, 28–34. doi: 10.1016/j.ijhm.2013.05.001

McCallaghan, S., Jackson, L. T. B., & Heyns, M. M. (2019). Transformational leadership, diversity climate, and job satisfaction in selected South African companies. *Journal of Psychology in Africa, 29*, 195–202. doi: 10.1080/14330237.2019.1619994

Melamed, S., Ben-Avi, I., Luz, J., & Green, M. S. (1995). Objective and subjective work monotony: Effects on job satisfaction, psychological distress, and absenteeism in blue-collar workers. *Journal of Applied Psychology, 80*, 29–42. doi: 10.1037/0021-9010.80.1.29

Menguc, B., Auh, S., Katsikeas, C. S., & Jung, Y. S. (2016). When does (mis)fit in customer orientation matter for frontline employees' job satisfaction and performance? *Journal of Marketing, 80*, 65–83. doi: 10.1509/jm.15.0327

Michel, J. S., Mitchelson, J. K., Kotrba, L. M., LeBreton, J. M., & Baltes, B. B. (2009). A comparative test of work-family conflict models and critical examination of work-family linkages. *Journal of Vocational Behavior, 74*, 199–218. doi: 10.1016/j.jvb.2008.12.005

Miller, B. K., Rutherford, M. A., & Kolodinsky, R. W. (2008). Perceptions of organizational politics: A meta-analysis of outcomes. *Journal of Business and Psychology, 22*, 209–222. doi: 10.1007/s10869-008-9061-5

Möhring, K., Naumann, E., Reifenscheid, M., Wenz, A., Rettig, T., Krieger, U., Friedel, S., Finkel, M., Cornesse, C., & Blom, A. G. (2021). The COVID-19 pandemic and subjective well-being: longitudinal evidence on satisfaction with work and family. *European Societies, 23*, S601–S617. doi: 10.1080/14616696.2020.1833066

Morganson, V. J., Major, D. A., Oborn, K. L., Verive, J. M., & Heelan, M. P. (2010). Comparing telework locations and traditional work arrangements: Differences in work-life balance support, job satisfaction, and inclusion. *Journal of Managerial Psychology, 25*, 578–595. doi: 10.1108/02683941011056941

Ng, T. W. H. (2017). Transformational leadership and performance outcomes: Analyses of multiple mediation pathways. *The Leadership Quarterly, 28*, 385–417. doi: 10.1016/j.leaqua.2016.11.008

Nielsen, M. B., & Einarsen, S. (2012). Outcomes of exposure to workplace bullying: A meta-analytic review. *Work & Stress, 26*, 309–332. doi: 10.1080/02678373.2012.734709

O'Connor, E., Peters, L., Rudolf, C., & Pooyan, A. (1982). Situational constraints and employee affective reactions: A partial field replication. *Group & Organization Management, 7*, 418–428.

Pearson, C. M., Andersson, L. M., & Porath, C. L. (2005). Workplace incivility. In S. Fox & P. E. Spector (Eds.), *Counterproductive work behavior: Investigations of actors and targets* (pp. 177–200). Washington, DC: American Psychological Association.

Peters, L. H., & O'Connor, E. J. (1980). Situational constraints and work outcomes: The influences of a frequently overlooked construct. *Academy of Management Review, 5*, 391–397.

Peters, L. H., O'Connor, E. J., & Rudolf, C. J. (1980). The behavioral and affective consequences of performance-relevant situational variables. *Organizational Behavior & Human Performance, 25*, 79–96.

Pierce, J. L., & Dunham, R. B. (1992). The 12-hour work day: A 48-hour, eight-day week. *Academy of Management Journal, 35*, 1086–1098. doi: 10.5465/256542

Pierce, J. L., & Newstrom, J. W. (1982). Employee responses to flexible work schedules: An inter-organization, inter-system comparison. *Journal of Management, 8*, 9–25. doi: 10.1177/014920638200800101

Pindek, S., & Spector, P. E. (2016). Organizational constraints: a meta-analysis of a major stressor. *Work & Stress, 30, 1–25.* doi: 10.1080/02678373.2015.1137376

Raggatt, P. T. F. (1991). Work stress among long-distance coach drivers: A survey and correlational study. *Journal of Organizational Behavior, 12*, 565–579. doi: 10.1002/job.4030120702

Ralston, D. A. (1989). The benefits of Flextime: Real or imagined? *Journal of Organizational Behavior, 10*, 369–373. doi: 10.1002/job.4030100407

Rice, R. W., Phillips, S. M., & McFarlin, D. B. (1990). Multiple discrepancies and pay satisfaction. *Journal of Applied Psychology, 75*, 386–393. doi: 10.1037/0021-9010.75.4.386

Rockstuhl, T., Dulebohn, J. H., Ang, S., & Shore, L. M. (2012). Leader-member exchange (LMX) and culture: A meta-analysis of correlates of LMX across 23 countries. *Journal of Applied Psychology, 97*, 1097–1130. doi: 10.1037/a0029978

Ronen, S., & Primps, S. B. (1981). The compressed work week as organizational change: Behavioral and attitudinal outcomes. *Academy of Management Review, 6*, 61–74. doi: 10.5465/amr.1981.4288003

Salancik, G., & Pfeffer, J. (1978). A social information processing approach to job attitudes and task design. *Administrative science quarterly, 23* 2, 224–253.

Schantz, A. D., Coxe, S., & Bruk-Lee, V. (2021). From where does my support come? Unpacking the contribution of support for police. *Policing: An International Journal, 44*, 343–360. doi: 10.1108/PIJPSM-07-2020-0130

Shepherd, W. J., Ployhart, R. E., & Kautz, J. (2020). The neglected role of collective customer perceptions in shaping collective employee satisfaction, service climate, voluntary turnover, and involuntary turnover: A cautionary note. *Journal of Applied Psychology, 105*, 1327–1337. doi: 10.1037/apl0000480. supp (Supplemental)

Shockley, K. M., Shen, W., DeNunzio, M. M., Arvan, M. L., & Knudsen, E. A. (2017). Disentangling the relationship between gender and work-family conflict: An integration of theoretical perspectives using meta-analytic methods. *Journal of Applied Psychology, 102*, 1601–1635. doi: 10.1037/apl0000246.supp (Supplemental)

Sims, H. P., Szilagyi, A. D., & Keller, R. T. (1976). The measurement of job characteristics. *Academy of Management Journal, 19*, 195–212. doi: 10.2307/255772

Smith, M. J., Hurrell, J. J. J., & Murphy, R. K., Jr. (1981). Stress and health effects in paced and unpaced work. In G. Salvendy & M. J. Smith (Eds.), *Machine pacing and occupational stress*. London: Taylor & Francis.

Spector, P. E. (1985). Higher-order need strength as a moderator of the job scope-employee outcome relationship: A meta-analysis. *Journal of Occupational Psychology, 58*, 119–127. doi: 10.1111/j.2044-8325.1985. tb00187.x

Spector, P. E. (1986). Perceived control by employees: A meta-analysis of studies concerning autonomy and participation at work. *Human Relations, 39*, 1005–1016. doi: 10.1177/001872678603901104

Spector, P. E. (1992). A consideration of the validity and meaning of self-report measures of job conditions. In C. L. Cooper & I. T. Robertson (Eds.), *International Review of Industrial and Organizational Psychology: 1992* (pp. 123–151). West Sussex: John Wiley.

Spector, P. E., & Jex, S. M. (1991). Relations of job characteristics from multiple data sources with employee affect, absence, turnover intentions, and health. *Journal of Applied Psychology, 76*, 46–53. doi: 10.1037/0021-9010.76.1.46

Stewart, W., & Barling, J. (1996). Fathers' work experiences effect children's behaviors via job-related affect and parenting behaviors. *Journal of Organizational Behavior, 17*, 221–232. doi: 10.1002/(SICI)1099-1379(199605)17:3<221::AID-JOB741>3.0.CO;2-G

Taber, T. D., & Taylor, E. (1990). A review and evaluation of the psychometric properties of the Job Diagnostic Survey. *Personnel Psychology, 43*, 467–500. doi: 10.1111/j.1744-6570.1990.tb02393.x

Tay, L., & Harter, J. K. (2013). Economic and labor market forces matter for worker well-being. *Applied Psychology: Health and Well-Being, 5*, 193–208. doi: 10.1111/aphw.12004

Thorsteinson, T. J. (2003). Job attitudes of part-time vs full-time workers: A meta-analytic review. *Journal of Occupational and Organizational Psychology, 76*, 151–177. doi: 10.1348/096317903765913687

Venkatesh, V., Ganster, D. C., Schuetz, S. W., & Sykes, T. A. (2021). Risks and rewards of conscientiousness during the COVID-19 pandemic. *Journal of Applied Psychology, 106*, 643–656. doi: 10.1037/apl0000919

Wall, T. D., Corbett, J., Martin, R., Clegg, C. W., & Jackson, P. R. (1990). Advanced manufacturing technology, work design, and performance: A change study. *Journal of Applied Psychology, 75*, 691–697. doi: 10.1037/0021-9010.75.6.691

Wang, Y.-D., & Hsieh, H.-H. (2012). Toward a better understanding of the link between ethical climate and job satisfaction: A multilevel analysis. *Journal of Business Ethics, 105*, 535–545. doi: 10.1007/s10551-011-0984-9

Warr, P., & Payne, R. (1983). Affective outcomes of paid employment in a random sample of British workers. *Journal of Occupational Behaviour, 4*, 91–104.

Way, S. A., Sturman, M. C., & Raab, C. (2010). What matters more?: Contrasting the effects of job satisfaction and service climate on hotel food and beverage managers' job performance. *Cornell Hospitality Quarterly, 51*, 379–397. doi: 10.1177/1938965510363783

Wegman, L. A., Hoffman, B. J., Carter, N. T., Twenge, J. M., & Guenole, N. (2018). Placing job characteristics in context: Cross-temporal meta-analysis of changes in job characteristics since 1975. *Journal of Management, 44*, 352–386. doi: 10.1177/0149206316654545

Yang, L.-Q., Caughlin, D. E., Gazica, M. W., Truxillo, D. M., & Spector, P. E. (2014). Workplace mistreatment climate and potential employee and organizational outcomes: A meta-analytic review from the target's perspective. *Journal of Occupational Health Psychology, 19*, 315–335. doi: 10.1037/a0036905

Yao, J., Lim, S., Guo, C. Y., Ou, A. Y., & Ng, J. W. X. (2021). Experienced incivility in the workplace: A meta-analytical review of its construct validity and nomological network. *Journal of Applied Psychology.* doi: 10.1037/apl0000870.supp (Supplemental)

Zohar, D. (2010). Thirty years of safety climate research: Reflections and future directions. *Accident Analysis and Prevention, 42,* 1517–1522.

5

PERSONALITY AND PERSON-JOB FIT

The importance of individual differences to the experience of job satisfaction was recognized as far back as the classic Hawthorne studies of the 1920s. In their writings about these studies conducted at the Western Electric Company, the researchers noted that certain individuals were chronically unhappy about their jobs (Roethlisberger, 1941). They called them the chronic kickers (an old term meaning complainer) in recognition of their constant complaints and the trait-like quality of job attitudes. It seemed that no matter how many times the researchers would fix a chronic kicker's complaint about the job, it wouldn't be long before there was a new complaint.

More recently, a series of studies with direct assessment of job satisfaction beginning with (Staw & Ross, 1985) noted that job satisfaction was stable over time, although more so for individuals remaining in the same job than taking new jobs (Dormann & Zapf, 2001). Further, job satisfaction along with other measures of well-being tends to get more stable with age as it is mainly younger workers who show fluctuation over time (Mäkikangas, Kinnunen, Feldt, & Schaufeli, 2016).

DOI: 10.4324/9781003250616-5

Even stronger evidence for the stability of job satisfaction was found in a 50-year lifespan longitudinal study that found job satisfaction could be predicted over a span of a lifetime. Staw, Bell, and Clausen (1986) analyzed data from the Intergenerational Studies begun at the University of California, Berkeley during the 1920s. Adolescents in this study were assessed using interviews, and follow-up questionnaires were given several times during their lives. The extensive material for each subject from adolescence was reviewed by clinicians who rated them on several personality traits, which were distilled into a single affective disposition score, that is, the extent to which they experienced negative emotions. Affective disposition in adolescence was found to significantly correlate with job satisfaction measured up to 50 years later in the follow-up questionnaires. Clearly there are factors within the individual that contribute to their job satisfaction.

Some have suggested that the trait-like nature of job satisfaction that produces consistency over time might be genetic. Evidence for a genetic component to consistency of job satisfaction comes from a study by Arvey, Bouchard, Segal, and Abraham (1989) who surveyed a group of identical twins reared separately. They estimated based on job satisfaction similarity within twin pairs that about 30% of the variance in job satisfaction is attributable to genetic factors. In other words, if one member of the twin was satisfied with their job, the other member was likely to feel the same about work. This is compelling evidence that there is some genetic component to job satisfaction, although the nature of the underlying process is unknown. It seems feasible that some individuals are predisposed to be happier in life, and this can affect job attitudes, but there are other possibilities. For example, perhaps differences between pairs of twins on innate aptitudes and capabilities can lead them to occupations that differ in satisfying characteristics.

Daily Fluctuation in Job Satisfaction

The research I have discussed so far considers job satisfaction to be something that varies among people, as if each person has their own level. Research has shown that it can be stable, and as Staw et al. (1986) showed, personality at a young age is related to satisfaction decades later. However, that job satisfaction scores might be related over time does not rule out daily fluctuation in satisfaction. Although people might not rate highly satisfied one day and highly dissatisfied the next, they might vary somewhat in the level of satisfaction (e.g., highly to moderately). One approach to the study of within-person fluctuation is the daily diary study. With these studies, people are asked to rate their job satisfaction one or more times per day for up to two weeks. Analyses can show how much employee satisfaction scores fluctuate day to day and what might predict that fluctuation.

Using that approach, Simbula (2010) estimated that about half the variation in job satisfaction scores is due to differences among employees (the stable component), and about half the variation is due to factors within the person (the unstable component). Some of the unstable part is certainly due to error variance—just random fluctuation in the ratings people make. On a 7-point scale, if my true level is 6.5, I will likely alternate between a 6 and a 7 randomly over time. But is some of that variability due to systematic factors such as events that occurred over the day?

Studies have shown that fluctuation in job satisfaction is associated with a variety of environmental and personal factors. For example, job satisfaction is related to the person's mood on the day of the survey (Niklas & Dormann, 2005); on days they are in a good mood they rate job satisfaction higher than on bad mood days. Job satisfaction also fluctuates with the level of job stressors encountered during the day, with lower satisfaction being reported on days of more stressors (Pindek, Arvan, & Spector, 2019). In the prior chapter I discussed how frequency of interpersonal conflicts at work was related to job satisfaction when studied between people. Within people on days that there are conflicts, job satisfaction has been shown to be lower than on days without conflict (Hagemeister & Volmer, 2018).

Job satisfaction can be relatively stable, especially for people whose job situation remains constant. There is also some degree of fluctuation that can occur day to day in response to events internal and external to the job. As people's working conditions change, as when switching jobs, job satisfaction is likely to be affected, particularly if those changes are significant. This might occur when a person quits a job that they find boring to take one that more closely matches their interests. This topic of person-job fit will be covered at the end of this chapter.

Personality Traits and Job Satisfaction

The above-mentioned studies have demonstrated that job satisfaction can be trait-like in that there is consistency over time in the level for individuals. Studies of individual personality traits offer clues about how personality affects job satisfaction. Although many traits have been shown to significantly correlate with job satisfaction, most research with personality has done little more than demonstrate relations without offering much theoretical explanation. Further, most research on personality and job satisfaction have focused on a narrow range of personality characteristics.

Five Factor Model

The study of personality has been dominated in recent decades by the Five Factor Model or Big Five. This taxonomy of personality traits places them into five broad factors of Agreeableness, Conscientiousness, Emotional Stability, Extraversion, and Openness to Experience (Digman, 1990). Meta-analyses have shown that job satisfaction relates to all but openness (Bruk-Lee, Khoury, Nixon, Goh, & Spector, 2009; Judge, Heller, & Mount, 2002).

Locus of Control

Locus of control is a cognitive variable that represents an individual's generalized belief in his or her ability to control positive and negative reinforcements in life. An external person believes in control by outside forces or people. An internal person believes that he or she can influence reinforcements. Most locus of control research has used general measures, such as that developed by Rotter (1966), that assess the extent to which people perceive control in their lives. In the work domain, Spector (1988) developed the Work Locus of Control Scale to assess how people feel concerning control of reinforcements only in the work place. That is, do they have control over what happens in their careers and in the workplace in general and not just in their current job situation.

There have been many studies that have found a significant correlation of locus of control with work variables including job satisfaction, with correlations being about twice as large for the work-specific measure than for measures of general locus of control (see meta-analysis by Wang,

Bowling, & Eschleman, 2010). These studies are mostly cross-sectional, showing that people who are internal in locus of control are more satisfied with their jobs than people who are external.

In a longitudinal study that is reminiscent of Staw et al. (1986), Spector and O'Connell (1994) followed a sample of college students as they started their working careers. They assessed personality including locus of control during students' final semester in school, and then followed up 18 months later to see how they felt about work. They found that locus of control assessed in college significantly correlated with job satisfaction measured on the job over a year later. Since locus of control was assessed prior to the students starting their jobs, the impact of the job on perceptions of locus of control can be ruled out.

Several mechanisms might account for the relation of locus of control and job satisfaction. Spector (1982) hypothesized that the relation between these two variables might be mediated by job performance. He noted that internals tend to perform their jobs better than externals, and if job performance is associated with rewards, satisfaction with the job might result. Thus, internals have higher job satisfaction because they benefit from the rewards of their better job performance.

Affective Traits

Two affective traits have been identified that reflect the experience of emotions across situations and time (Watson, Clark, & Tellegen, 1988). Negative affectivity (NA) is the tendency to experience negative emotions, whereas positive affectivity (PA) is the tendency to experience positive emotions. It has been suggested that these personality characteristics affect how people perceive and respond to the world. They have both been shown to link to job satisfaction, with NA being negatively and PA being positively related to global job satisfaction (Bruk-Lee et al., 2009). This is also the case with individual facets from the JDI (coworkers, pay, promotion, supervision, and work itself), with work itself having the strongest relationship with both affective traits (Bowling, Hendricks, & Wagner, 2008).

As with locus of control, it is important to understand why affective traits correlate with job satisfaction. Several mechanisms have been suggested for at least the NA side. Moyle (1995) hypothesized that high NA people tend to perceive their job situation in negative ways, which leads them to experience job dissatisfaction. Spector, Jex, and Chen (1995) found evidence that it was not just perceptions, but that people who were high in NA were in jobs with less favorable job characteristics that are related to job satisfaction. Watson, Pennebaker, and Folger (1986) felt that NA contaminates many organizational measures, including measures of job satisfaction. They suggested that correlations between job satisfaction and other organizational variables assessed through employee questionnaires were due to the influence of NA on responses to surveys. Research on this possibility finds little support that NA is the explanation for correlations of organizational variables with job satisfaction (Moyle, 1995; Spector, Zapf, Chen, & Frese, 2000; Williams, Gavin, & Williams, 1996).

Person-Job Fit

Most of the research discussed in this book so far has investigated characteristics of the job and characteristics of the person separately. Some research has looked at the interaction between job and person factors to see if certain types of people respond differently to certain types of jobs. This person-job fit approach posits that there will be job satisfaction when characteristics of the job are matched to characteristics of the person (Edwards, 1991). One such idea is contained in the job characteristics theory (Hackman & Oldham, 1976), which hypothesized a role for growth need strength, as I discussed in the previous chapter.

One stream of research that has taken the person-job fit perspective has looked at the discrepancy between what people say they want on the job and what they have. For example, a person might be asked how much skill variety there is on the job versus how much skill variety is wanted. The smaller the discrepancy, the higher should be the job satisfaction. Studies that have used this procedure have generally found that discrepancy relates to job satisfaction as expected (Edwards, 1991).

A different approach has been taken in many of the job characteristics studies that investigated the hypothesized role of growth need strength or GNS. In job characteristics studies, growth need strength is treated as a moderator of the relation between job characteristics and job satisfaction; that is, people high in GNS will respond favorably to a high-scope job, while their counterparts who are low in GNS will not. As noted in Chapter 4, meta-analyses have found support for the moderator effect with both global and facet satisfaction (Loher, Noe, Moeller, & Fitzgerald, 1985; Spector, 1985). The correlation between job characteristics and job satisfaction was higher for individuals high on GNS than for individuals low on GNS.

Vocational Interest Fit

Research on vocational interests provides more evidence that the fit of the person to the job is important for job satisfaction. Much of this research is based on Holland's (1959) theory that led to the development of a six-dimension taxonomy of vocational interests. The RIASEC model consists of the following dimensions that reflect vocational personalities (Harper, 2020):

- **Realistic**: Prefers to work with concrete things rather than people. Likes physical activities.
- **Investigative**: Prefers to solve complex problems and work with information and reasoning.
- **Artistic**: Prefers to do things involving creativity and innovation. Does not like following rules.
- **Social**: Prefers activities involving interacting with and helping others.
- **Enterprising**: Prefers influencing and leading others.
- **Conventional**: Prefers jobs with rules and structured activities. Such people are methodical and organized.

Presumably, individuals whose jobs are best matched to their personalities will be most satisfied. For example, a person high on investigative type would be happiest if their job tasks involved researching things, for example, as a police detective or scientist. In an extensive review of the vast literature on Holland's model, Spokane, Meir, and Catalano (2000) concluded that match between people's vocational interests and their jobs was associated with job satisfaction. They also noted that many studies used an imprecise method of using job titles or job types to match the person's interests to the job rather than the specific characteristics of job tasks the person had. It follows that a more precise method of matching personality to the specific tasks a person performed on the job (as opposed to the title of their job) would yield stronger relationships between fit and job satisfaction.

Overqualification

As noted earlier, the fit between personality and the job, and vocational interests and the job are related to job satisfaction. Another aspect of fit has to do with the fit of a person's background, knowledge, and skill with the job. Of particular concern in job markets with limited job choices is over-qualification when job holders have more education, knowledge and skill than needed in the job. It is assumed that those who are overqualified will be dissatisfied because of a lack of fit with the job. Indeed research shows that perceptions of being overqualified are associated with being bored (Andel, Pindek, & Arvan, 2021) and dissatisfied (mean correlation of = 0.36 in a meta-analysis by Harari, Manapragada, & Viswesvaran, 2017) at work.

A limitation to most studies is that the measure of overqualification is based on employee ratings and merely establishes that perceptions of the job are related to job satisfaction. Arvan, Pindek, Andel, and Spector (2019) went a step farther and measured not only perceived overqualification, but objective overqualification based on matching education and skill levels to those required in the job. They studied recent college graduates all of whom had the same level of education but varied in the education level required in their jobs. Consistent with the Harari et al. (2017) meta-analysis, there was a -0.38 correlation between perceived overqualification and job satis-faction. There was also a 0.54 correlation between objective overqualifica-tion and perceived overqualification. However, there was a nonsignificant (-0.11) correlation between objective overqualification and job satisfaction. This study questions the assumption that people who are overqualified in having too much education or skill will be bored and unhappy with their jobs. In a second study they found evidence that job satisfaction was the antecedent rather than the effect of perceived overqualification, suggesting that people who are unhappy with the job rate themselves as overqualified. Taken together both studies suggest that being objectively overqualified might not have much impact on job satisfaction, but job satisfaction might have an impact on how people view their jobs.

Job Crafting

When a job is not a good fit to an employee's interests or skills, it is often possible for the person to re-engineer or craft their job to make it more interesting and challenging, or to make it less demanding (Tims, Bakker, & Derks, 2015). Often supervisors will allow enough discretion that allows for at least some job crafting. It can involve a number of activities such as (Tims, Bakker, & Derks, 2012)

- Learn new things at work.
- Decide how to do tasks.
- Avoid people who might upset you.
- Seek feedback from supervisors.
- Ask colleagues for advice.
- Volunteer for interesting tasks.

Some of the job crafting activities can be forms of organizational citizenship behavior (to be discussed in Chapter 6) which are behaviors that go beyond core tasks. Others have more to do with controlling the amount of time spent on tasks, with more time on interesting activities and less time on boring or stressful activities.

Job crafting is associated with job autonomy (Rudolph, Katz, Lavigne, & Zacher, 2017), which is not surprising as it requires latitude in how to perform the job to be able to job craft. It is also related to work engagement which reflects the level of motivation an employee has for the job (Shin, Hur, & Choi, 2020). Finally, participating in job crafting is associated with having high job satisfaction (Llorente-Alonso & Topa, 2019; Zhang & Li, 2020). Whether job crafting leads to engagement and satisfaction or the reverse is not clear from these studies. Some evidence that crafting might be an antecedent of engagement can be found in intervention studies in which employees who are encouraged to job craft show increases in engagement (Oprea, Barzin, Vîrgă, Iliescu, & Rusu, 2019). That employees who increase crafting activities become more engaged, does not rule out the possibility that engagement leads employees to spontaneously job craft on their own without encouragement.

Living a Calling at Work

One aspect of person-job fit is when a person is living their calling through work. A calling is simply the sense of overall meaning and purpose people have in life that motivates them to contribute to the common good (Duffy,

Dik, Douglass, England, & Velez, 2018). When a job enables a person to live their calling, he or she should find that job to be fulfilling and motivating, thus leading to job satisfaction. Indeed studies have shown that living a calling through work is associated with job satisfaction (e.g., Ehrhardt & Ensher, 2021).

There is a potential downside to having a calling, however. As Duffy, Douglass, Autin, England, and Dik (2016) explain, there are two problems with having a calling. First, if a person has a job that fits their calling, he or she is vulnerable to overworking and workaholism that can lead to burnout. They tested this idea in a sample of employed adults and counter to the overwork hypothesis, living a calling was negatively, not positively, associated with burnout. Further, they found that the negative effect of burnout on job satisfaction was less for those living their callings. Thus, individuals who were living their calling at work did not become as dissatisfied when hard work led to burnout.

Second, what happens when a person has a calling but is unable to live it at work? Gazica and Spector (2015) addressed this question in a sample of college professors. Each was classified as having a calling that they were living at work, having a calling they were not living at work, and having no calling. They found as expected that faculty living their calling were higher in job and life satisfaction than the other two groups. Those living their calling as well as those with no calling were lower on emotional and physical strains. However, those having a calling but not living it were lower on both satisfactions and higher on both strains. This suggests that having a calling is a two-edged sword. If you can live it at work, there is a well-being benefit, but not being able to live it results in decreased satisfaction and increased strain.

Through much of the calling literature it is assumed that living a calling leads to job satisfaction. Studies that find a positive relationship between living a calling and job satisfaction support that idea, but cross-sectional studies are unable to shed light on direction of effects. Duffy, Allan, Autin, and Douglass (2014) addressed the directionality issue in a three-wave study of calling and job satisfaction over a six-month period. Their complex modeling found evidence that more likely job satisfaction led to calling rather than the reverse. They suggest that calling is a dynamic process and that finding oneself in a satisfying job can lead to that job becoming a calling over time.

References

Andel, S., Pindek, S., & Arvan, M. L. (2021). Bored, angry, and overqualified? The high- and low-intensity pathways linking perceived overqualification to behavioural outcomes. *European Journal of Work and Organizational Psychology*. doi: 10.1080/1359432X.2021.1919624

Arvan, M. L., Pindek, S., Andel, S. A., & Spector, P. E. (2019). Too good for your job? Disentangling the relationships between objective overqualification, perceived overqualification, and job dissatisfaction. *Journal of Vocational Behavior, 115*, 103323. doi: 10.1016/j.jvb.2019.103323

Arvey, R. D., Bouchard, T., Segal, N., & Abraham, L. M. (1989). Job satisfaction: Environmental and genetic components. *Journal of Applied Psychology, 74*, 187–192.

Bowling, N. A., Hendricks, E. A., & Wagner, S. H. (2008). Positive and negative affectivity and facet satisfaction: A meta-analysis. *Journal of Business and Psychology, 23*, 115–125. doi: 10.1007/s10869-008-9082-0

Bruk-Lee, V., Khoury, H. A., Nixon, A. E., Goh, A., & Spector, P. E. (2009). Replicating and extending past personality/job satisfaction meta-analyses. *Human Performance, 22*, 156–189. doi: 10.1080/08959280902743709

Digman, J. M. (1990). Personality structure: Emergence of the five-factor model. *Annual Review of Psychology, 41*, 417–440.

Dormann, C., & Zapf, D. (2001). Job satisfaction: A meta-analysis of stabilities. *Journal of Organizational Behavior, 22*, 483–504. doi: 10.1002/job.98

Duffy, R. D., Allan, B. A., Autin, K. L., & Douglass, R. P. (2014). Living a calling and work well-being: A longitudinal study. *Journal of Counseling Psychology, 61*, 605–615. doi: 10.1037/cou0000042

Duffy, R. D., Dik, B. J., Douglass, R. P., England, J. W., & Velez, B. L. (2018). Work as a calling: A theoretical model. *Journal of Counseling Psychology, 65*, 423–439. doi: 10.1037/cou0000276

Duffy, R. D., Douglass, R. P., Autin, K. L., England, J., & Dik, B. J. (2016). Does the dark side of a calling exist? Examining potential negative effects. *The Journal of Positive Psychology, 11*, 634–646. doi: 10.1080/17439760.2015.1137626

Edwards, J. R. (1991). Person-job fit: A conceptual integration, literature review, and methodological critique. In C. L. Cooper & I. T. Robertson (Eds.), *International review of industrial and organizational psychology, Vol. 6* (pp. 283–357). Oxford, England: John Wiley & Sons.

Ehrhardt, K., & Ensher, E. (2021). Perceiving a calling, living a calling, and calling outcomes: How mentoring matters. *Journal of Counseling Psychology, 68*, 168–181. doi: 10.1037/cou0000513

Gazica, M. W., & Spector, P. E. (2015). A comparison of individuals with unanswered callings to those with no calling at all. *Journal of Vocational Behavior, 91*, 1–10. doi: 10.1016/j.jvb.2015.08.008

Hackman, J. R., & Oldham, G. R. (1976). Motivation through design of work – Test of a theory. *Organizational Behavior and Human Performance, 16*, 250–279. doi: 10.1016/0030-5073(76)90016-7

Hagemeister, A., & Volmer, J. (2018). Do social conflicts at work affect employees' job satisfaction?: The moderating role of emotion regulation. *International Journal of Conflict Management, 29*, 213–235. doi: 10.1108/ IJCMA-11-2016-0097

Harari, M. B., Manapragada, A., & Viswesvaran, C. (2017). Who thinks they're a big fish in a small pond and why does it matter? A meta-analysis of perceived overqualification. *Journal of Vocational Behavior, 102*, 28–47. doi: 10.1016/j.jvb.2017.06.002

Harper, H. (2020). How are you intelligent? An introduction to the Holland codes (RIASEC), from https://www.thecareerproject.org/blog/ how-are-you-intelligent-an-introduction-to-the-holland-codes-riasec/

Holland, J. L. (1959). A theory of vocational choice. *Journal of Counseling Psychology, 6*, 35–45. doi: 10.1037/h0040767

Judge, T. A., Heller, D., & Mount, M. K. (2002). Five-factor model of personality and job satisfaction: A meta-analysis. *Journal of Applied Psychology, 87*, 530–541. doi: 10.1037/0021-9010.87.3.530

Llorente-Alonso, M., & Topa, G. (2019). Individual crafting, collaborative crafting, and job satisfaction: The mediator role of engagement. *Journal of Work and Organizational Psychology, 35*, 217–226. doi: 10.5093/ jwop2019a23

Loher, B. T., Noe, R. A., Moeller, N. L., & Fitzgerald, M. P. (1985). A meta-analysis of the relation of job characteristics to job satisfaction. *Journal of Applied Psychology, 70*, 280–289. doi: 10.1037/0021-9010.70.2.280

Mäkikangas, A., Kinnunen, U., Feldt, T., & Schaufeli, W. (2016). The longitudinal development of employee well-being: A systematic review. *Work & Stress, 30*, 46–70. doi: 10.1080/02678373.2015.1126870

Moyle, P. (1995). The role of negative affectivity in the stress process: Tests of alternative models. *Journal of Organizational Behavior, 16*, 647–668.

Niklas, C. D., & Dormann, C. (2005). The impact of state affect on job satisfaction. *European Journal of Work and Organizational Psychology, 14*, 367–388. doi: 10.1080/13594320500348880

Oprea, B. T., Barzin, L., Vîrgă, D., Iliescu, D., & Rusu, A. (2019). Effectiveness of job crafting interventions: A meta-analysis and utility analysis. *European Journal of Work and Organizational Psychology, 28*, 723–741. doi: 10.1080/1359432X.2019.1646728

Pindek, S., Arvan, M. L., & Spector, P. E. (2019). The stressor-strain relationship in diary studies: A meta-analysis of the within and between levels. *Work & Stress, 33*, 1–21. doi: 10.1080/02678373.2018.1445672

Roethlisberger, F. J. (1941). *Management and morale*. Cambridge, MA: Harvard University Press.

Rotter, J. B. (1966). Generalized expectancies for internal versus external control of reinforcement. *Psychological Monographs: General & Applied, 80*(1), 1–28.

Rudolph, C. W., Katz, I. M., Lavigne, K. N., & Zacher, H. (2017). Job crafting: A meta-analysis of relationships with individual differences, job characteristics, and work outcomes. *Journal of Vocational Behavior, 102*, 112–138. doi: 10.1016/j.jvb.2017.05.008

Shin, Y., Hur, W.-M., & Choi, W.-H. (2020). Coworker support as a double-edged sword: A moderated mediation model of job crafting, work engagement, and job performance. *The International Journal of Human Resource Management, 31*, 1417–1438. doi: 10.1080/09585192.2017.1407352

Simbula, S. (2010). Daily fluctuations in teachers' well-being: A diary study using the Job Demands–Resources model. *Anxiety, Stress & Coping: An International Journal, 23*, 563–584. doi: 10.1080/10615801003728273

Spector, P. E. (1982). Behavior in organizations as a function of employee's locus of control. *Psychological Bulletin, 91*, 482–497. doi: 10.1037/0033-2909.91.3.482

Spector, P. E. (1985). Higher-order need strength as a moderator of the job scope-employee outcome relationship: A meta-analysis. *Journal of Occupational Psychology, 58*, 119–127. doi: 10.1111/j.2044-8325.1985.tb00187.x

Spector, P. E. (1988). Development of the Work Locus of Control Scale. *Journal of Occupational Psychology, 61*, 335–340. doi: 10.1111/j.2044-8325.1988.tb00470.x

Spector, P. E., Jex, S. M., & Chen, P. Y. (1995). Relations of incumbent affect-related personality traits with incumbent and objective measures of characteristics of jobs. *Journal of Organizational Behavior, 16*, 59–65. doi: 10.1002/job.4030160108

Spector, P. E., & O'Connell, B. J. (1994). The contribution of personality traits, negative affectivity, locus of control and type A to the subsequent reports of job stressors and job strains. *Journal of Occupational and Organizational Psychology, 67*, 1–12. doi: 10.1111/j.2044-8325.1994.tb00545.x

Spector, P. E., Zapf, D., Chen, P. Y., & Frese, M. (2000). Why negative affectivity should not be controlled in job stress research: Don't throw out the baby with the bath water. *Journal of Organizational Behavior, 21*, 79–95. doi: 10.1002/%28SICI%291099-1379%28200002%2921:1%3C79::AID-JOB964%3E3.0.CO;2-G

Spokane, A. R., Meir, E. I., & Catalano, M. (2000). Person-environment congruence and Holland's theory: A review and reconsideration. *Journal of Vocational Behavior, 57*, 137–187. doi: 10.1006/jvbe.2000.1771

Staw, B. M., Bell, N. E., & Clausen, J. A. (1986). The dispositional approach to job attitudes: A lifetime longitudinal test. [Empirical study; longitudinal study]. *Administrative Science Quarterly, 31*, 56–77. doi: 10.2307/2392766

Staw, B. M., & Ross, J. (1985). Stability in the midst of change: A dispositional approach to job attitudes. [Empirical study; longitudinal study]. *Journal of Applied Psychology, 70*, 469–480. doi: 10.1037/0021-9010.70.3.469

Tims, M., Bakker, A. B., & Derks, D. (2012). Development and validation of the job crafting scale. *Journal of Vocational Behavior, 80*, 173–186. doi: 10.1016/j.jvb.2011.05.009

Tims, M., Bakker, A. B., & Derks, D. (2015). Examining Job crafting from an interpersonal perspective: Is employee job crafting related to the well-being of colleagues? *Applied Psychology, 64*, 727–753. doi: 10.1111/apps.12043

Wang, Q., Bowling, N. A., & Eschleman, K. J. (2010). A meta-analytic examination of work and general locus of control. *Journal of Applied Psychology, 95*, 761–768. doi: 10.1037/a0017707.supp (Supplemental)

Watson, D., Clark, L. A., & Tellegen, A. (1988). Development and validation of brief measures of positive and negative affect: The PANAS scales. *Journal of Personality and Social Psychology, 54*, 1063–1070. doi: 10.1037/0022-3514.54.6.1063

Watson, D., Pennebaker, J. W., & Folger, R. (1986). Beyond negative affectivity: Measuring stress and satisfaction in the workplace. *Journal of Organizational Behavior Management, 8*, 141–157. doi: 10.1300/J075v08n02_09

Williams, L. J., Gavin, M. B., & Williams, M. L. (1996). Measurement and nonmeasurement processes with negative affectivity and employee attitudes. *Journal of Applied Psychology, 81*, 88–101. doi: 10.1037/0021-9010.81.1.88

Zhang, T., & Li, B. (2020). Job crafting and turnover intention: The mediating role of work engagement and job satisfaction. *Social Behavior and Personality: An International Journal, 48*, 1–9.

6

BEHAVIOR AND PERFORMANCE

There are many behaviors that are related to job satisfaction. Some contribute to the organization in a positive way and others can be counterproductive. Some of those counterproductive behaviors involve actively engaging in behaviors destructive to organizations and other people, whereas others are more passive forms of work avoidance. Taken together these different types of employee behaviors contribute to an organization's effectiveness.

Job Performance

Conventional wisdom says that job satisfaction should be related to job performance. After all, a happy employee should be a motivated and productive employee. Studies have established that the correlation between these two variables is rather modest, with mean correlations below 0.30 (Bowling, Khazon, Meyer, & Burrus, 2015; Judge, Thoresen, Bono, & Patton, 2001). These meta-analyses established that job performance and job satisfaction correlate with one another, at least to a moderate extent.

DOI: 10.4324/9781003250616-6

However, they do little to explain the reasons for observed correlations. Although it is possible that job satisfaction leads to job performance, the opposite direction of causality is also equally feasible. People who are happy with their jobs might be more motivated, work harder, and therefore perform better. There is some evidence that people who perform better like their jobs better because of the rewards that are often associated with good performance.

One indication that performance leads to satisfaction comes from a study by Jacobs and Solomon (1977). They hypothesized that the correlation between job satisfaction and job performance would be higher in jobs where good performance was rewarded than in jobs where it was not. Under such conditions employees who perform well get rewards, and rewards should lead to job satisfaction. Consistent with their predictions, Jacobs and Solomon found that job performance and job satisfaction were more strongly correlated when organizations tied rewards to good job performance.

Caldwell and O'Reilly (1990) provided indirect evidence that job performance can lead to job satisfaction. They showed that matching employee abilities to job requirements enhances job performance. They also found that matching employee abilities to job requirements enhances job satisfaction, as well. People who are better able to do their jobs well and perform well tend to have higher job satisfaction. It seems likely that job satisfaction is caused by job performance at least in part, although this relation might be explained by the rewards given to individuals who perform well. It is also possible that people who have better person-job fit (as described in Chapter 5) are more satisfied because the job is a better match to their talents.

Customer Service

For customer facing employees, job performance is about customer service because customer service is what drives sales. An important question concerns whether the job satisfaction of customer service employees affects the quality of service they provide and the customer experience. Can a dissatisfied employee appear cheerful and engaged in customer service encounters, or will their dissatisfaction with the job negatively affect service encounters as customers sense their unhappiness?

The first question about job satisfaction of customer service employees is whether it is related to their performance. In a meta-analysis, Franke and Park (2006) found that job satisfaction of employees is associated with good job performance as indicated by both self-ratings and supervisor-ratings, as well as sales numbers. The second question is whether the attitudes of salespeople affect the customer experience. Studies have shown that job satisfaction of the salesperson is positively related to customer perceptions of service quality (Benitez & Medina, 2021; Brown & Lam, 2008) and customer satisfaction (Brown & Lam, 2008; Harter, Schmidt, & Hayes, 2002). Combined these studies underscore that it is particularly important for customer service employees to be satisfied with their jobs, as that satisfaction affects not only how well they perform job tasks, but also the outcomes of that performance.

Organizational Performance

The bottom-line question for managers is whether job satisfaction affects the bottom-line performance of organizations themselves. If employees who are satisfied perform better, does that performance translate into performance outcomes at the organization level? Studies have been conducted at the organization level to address this question in seeing whether the average correlation among employees within an organization, or unit of an organization, relates to overall organizational performance.

These studies have shown that organizations or units that have more satisfied employees have better outcomes, including:

- Client satisfaction (Taris & Schreurs, 2009) and customer satisfaction (Harter et al., 2002; Koys, 2001).
- Earnings per share of company stock (Schneider, Hanges, Smith, & Salvaggio, 2003).
- Profitability (Harter et al., 2002; Koys, 2001).

Showing that job satisfaction and organizational effectiveness are related is only one part of the story. The other is whether job satisfaction might lead to effectiveness or is the byproduct of effectiveness. Both are probably the case, as longitudinal studies that assess employee satisfaction and organizational performance over a period of several years find evidence for each direction of effects (Kessler, Lucianetti, Pindek, Zhu, & Spector, 2020; Schneider et al., 2003). Koys (2001) studied the issue looking at individual restaurants in a national chain and found more evidence that job satisfaction led to organizational performance than the reverse.

Organizational Citizenship Behavior (OCB)

Organizational citizenship behavior or OCB is behavior by an employee that helps coworkers or the organization. OCB is behavior that goes beyond the formal requirements of a job or what might be written into a job description (Organ, 1997). What makes such behavior OCB is that it is not part of the individual's assigned responsibilities, although there are times that supervisors might make it clear they expect a certain amount of OCB that goes beyond what the employee considers their core job (Vigoda-Gadot, 2006). Examples of OCB behaviors, from the Organizational Citizenship Behavior Checklist or OCB-C (Fox, Spector, Goh, Bruursema, & Kessler, 2012) include:

- Take time to advise or mentor a coworker.
- Help a coworker learn a new skill.
- Offer suggestions to improve how work is done.
- Help a coworker who has too much to do.
- Give up a break to complete work.

As discussed above, the relationship of job satisfaction with job performance is lower than might be expected, and at least some of that relationship might be due to performance leading to satisfaction. However, it could be that job satisfaction leads to OCB rather than task performance. This is because people likely have more control over the extra tasks that they do than the main portion of their jobs. Meta-analyses of OCB find that it does correlate with job performance, but the magnitude of correlation is not much different from job performance (Carpenter, Berry, & Houston, 2014; Organ & Ryan, 1995).

There are questions, however, about whether OCB relates to job satisfaction due to methodological flaws in the measurement of OCB in most studies. Many OCB instruments contain items that overlap with measures of counterproductive work behavior or CWB (Dalal, 2005) that I discuss next. This overlap makes it difficult to determine if the correlations found between OCB and job satisfaction are due to OCB or to CWB. Studies using OCB instruments that do not contain CWB content have found few significant correlations with job satisfaction (Fox et al., 2012; Spector, Bauer, & Fox, 2010; Spector & Che, 2014). Perhaps satisfied employees are no more likely to engage in OCB than their dissatisfied colleagues. Satisfied employees might engage in OCB because they are motivated and want to help their employers and coworkers. On the other hand, dissatisfied employees might engage in OCB as a means of escaping job tasks that they do not enjoy. If both suggestions are true, we would not expect to find that job satisfaction relates to OCB because both satisfied and dissatisfied employees engage in it, although for different reasons.

Counterproductive Work Behavior (CWB)

In some ways the opposite of organizational citizenship behavior is counterproductive work behavior or CWB. It consists of acts committed by an employee that either intentionally or unintentionally hurts the organization or people in the organization (Spector & Fox, 2005). This includes aggression against coworkers or the employer, sabotage, and theft. These behaviors can have many causes, but often they are associated with dissatisfaction and other negative feelings at work.

Studies have shown that some of the same variables linked to job satisfaction are also linked to CWB. These include organizational constraints (Pindek & Spector, 2016), perceived unfairness (Berry, Carpenter, & Barratt, 2012), role ambiguity and conflict (Zhang, Crant, & Weng, 2019), social stressors (Bowling & Beehr, 2006), and negative emotions (Berry et al., 2012). CWB is also related to job satisfaction, with dissatisfied employees being more likely to engage in CWB as reported by themselves (Hershcovis et al., 2007) and others (Berry et al., 2012).

CWB does not always occur in response to stressors and negative emotions at work. An important factor involved in these behaviors is control at work. Individuals who believe they have control are less likely to commit these acts than individuals who believe they have no control (Spector, 1997). Storms and Spector (1987) reported that locus of control moderated the relation of frustration at work with several forms of CWB. Externals who believe outside forces control their outcomes, but not internals who believe in personal control, showed a relation between feelings of frustration and reports of CWB.

As you have seen throughout this book with other variables, it is not entirely clear about the role job satisfaction might play in CWB. It is well established across many studies that the two are related, but the reasons are not entirely clear. It is possible that people who dislike their jobs are using CWB to get back at their employers. On the other hand, job satisfaction reflects either poor conditions at work or a poor person-job fit, and those situations might serve as a trigger for CWB rather than the dissatisfaction itself.

Cyberloafing

Modern technology has provided employees with a new way to avoid work. Employees can spend work time answering personal e-mails, making online purchases, or watching entertaining videos. These are examples of workplace cyberloafing when an employee uses computer devices for nonwork activities during work time (Lim, 2002). As Lim explains, there has been a lot of concern among leaders of organizations about cyberloafing reducing employee productivity. This has led some companies to restrict cyberloafing both with policies prohibiting it, and by limiting access to the internet on company devices. But is the concern justified?

Early research on cyberloafing approached it as a form of CWB (Lim, 2002). It was assumed that some of the same factors that led to CWB also led to cyberloafing such as injustice (Blau, Yang, & Ward-Cook, 2006) and stress (Henle & Blanchard, 2008). Based on this view, we would expect that cyberloafing would be negatively related to job satisfaction. Employees who are dissatisfied with their jobs might retaliate against their employers with cyberloafing as a form of CWB.

Research done more recently has failed to support the CWB view of cyberloafing, and instead suggests it is a complex phenomenon. A meta-analysis of 14 studies found little relationship of cyberloafing with job performance (Mercado, Giordano, & Dilchert, 2017), which shows that the concern with employees neglecting their jobs while cyberloafing is unfounded. Further, the relationship between cyberloafing and job satisfaction has varied across studies. Although some studies have found the expected negative correlation

(Andel, Kessler, Pindek, Kleinman, & Spector, 2019; Cook, 2017), others have found a positive correlation (Öztürk, Dömbekci, & Yesildal, 2018). On the positive side, there is evidence that cyberloafing can serve as a coping mechanism that provides a break from boredom and stress (Pindek, Krajcevska, & Spector, 2018). Andel et al. (2019) found an overall negative correlation of cyberloafing with job satisfaction, but that cyberloafing and stress interacted. Under conditions of low stress employees who cyberloafed were less satisfied than employees who did not. Under conditions of high stress, however, employees who cyberloafed were more satisfied with their jobs. An implication of these findings is that people are more satisfied at work if they are able to cyberloaf to cope with stress (Weissenfeld, Abramova, & Krasnova, 2019).

Withdrawal Behavior

Many theories hypothesize that people who dislike their jobs will avoid them, either permanently by quitting or temporarily by being absent or coming in late. Job satisfaction is a central variable in almost every theory of withdrawal behavior. Mitra, Jenkins, and Gupta (1992) noted that many researchers consider absence and turnover to be related phenomena that have the same underlying motivations to escape a dissatisfying job.

A meta-analysis found that absence and turnover were significantly intercorrelated (Mitra et al., 1992). Employees who quit a job were likely to have had higher levels of absence just prior to leaving the job than did employees who did not quit. However, this relation does not necessarily mean that absence and turnover are alternative reactions to job dissatisfaction. On many jobs people lose their pool of sick leave upon leaving, which might motivate someone about to quit a job to consume their sick leave rather than lose it. They might also be absent because of job interviews preceding their quitting. Reasons for missing work might be quite different for employees who do not quit.

Absence

Absence is a phenomenon that can reduce organizational effectiveness and efficiency by lost productivity and increased labor costs. On many jobs floaters or substitutes are required for each absent employee. The employee might continue to get paid, resulting in increased costs from paying both the employee and a short-term replacement. Not surprisingly, organizations are concerned about absence.

Conventional wisdom suggests that job satisfaction would lead to absence, and indeed models of absence often suggest that job dissatisfaction plays a critical role in an employee's decision to be absent (e.g., Mayfield, Mayfield, & Ma, 2020). People who dislike their jobs should be expected to avoid coming to work. However, empirical support for this position has been surprisingly difficult to find. Correlations between job satisfaction and absence have been inconsistent across studies and mean correlations from meta-analyses have been very small (Bowling & Hammond, 2008).

At least one statistical reason for the small correlations between job satisfaction and absence is the distribution of absences across employees (Hammer & Landau, 1981). In most samples the distribution of absences is extremely skewed, with few employees having many instances of absence. A typical absence distribution from a sample of employees is shown in Figure 6.1. As you can see, 60% of the employees were not absent at all, and another quarter of them were absent only once. The severe nonnormality of absence distributions like this one can make it difficult to find a correlation of absence with another variable like job satisfaction. Hammer and Landau

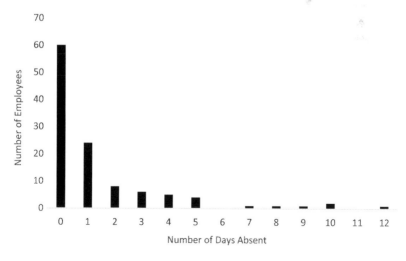

Figure 6.1 A typical distribution of three-month employee absences from an organization.

note that correlation might not be the best statistic to use for absence data, because the required assumptions of normally distributed observations are too badly violated. This means that the correlation coefficient is difficult to interpret, requiring the use of other data analysis techniques.

It also seems likely that the correlation between job satisfaction and absence is not bigger because absence is a complex phenomenon that can have multiple causes (Kohler & Mathieu, 1993). A person might be absent because of being ill, a family member being ill, being fatigued, or having to conduct personal business, as well as just not wanting to go to work. The first four reasons have little to do with job satisfaction. Clearly, the reason for absence should be considered if we are going to understand the role of job satisfaction.

Dalton and Mesch (1991) demonstrated that the reasons for absence impacted its correlates. They classified absence into absence due to illness versus absence due to other causes. Absence due to illness was significantly correlated with job satisfaction, but absence due to other causes was not. It was related to absence policies and tenure. The less restrictive the policy and the longer the tenure, the more the absence.

Job satisfaction may have played a central role in research on absence, but it has been replaced over time by other more important variables. For example, Goff and Jamison (1990) found that having primary childcare responsibilities predicted absence much better than did job satisfaction. Having to take care of children is a reason for absence that is more important than disliking the job. Haccoun and tale Jeanrie (1995) reported larger correlations (as high as 0.37) between absence and attitudes tolerant of absence than are typically found for job satisfaction.

Farrell and Stamm (1988) found in their meta-analysis of 72 studies that the two best correlates of absence were prior history of absence and organizational absence control policies, with mean correlations of 0.47 and −0.30, respectively. Organizations that have lax absence policies will have more absence, especially from individuals who have tendencies to stay home from work. Those tendencies can be affected by individual differences. For example, the tendency to experience guilt from doing something wrong is a personality characteristic that has been shown to predict absence. Those who are high on the trait are less likely to stay out of work, presumably because they would feel guilty about it (Schaumberg & Flynn, 2017).

One additional factor that may lead to absence is what Nicholson and Johns (1985) called the absence culture of an organization or work group. When norms of a work group support absence, there will be high levels. Conversely, when the norms of the group discourage absence, there will be low levels. Several studies support the idea that organizations have cultures that determine absence. For example, Mathieu and Kohler (1990) found that individuals tended to have more absences if they were in work groups where members were absent frequently. Martocchio (1994) showed that coworker reports of absence costs and benefits predicted the absences of individuals. These norms that affect individual decisions to be absent can occur within individual workgroups, entire organizations, and even countries where absence rates can differ tremendously.

There is another way in which factors external to the organization can affect absence. Mitra et al. (1992) conducted a meta-analysis in which they demonstrated that the unemployment rates for the times during which data were collected in studies affected the job satisfaction-absence relationship. The correlation coefficients tended to be higher when data were collected during times of low unemployment than during periods of high unemployment. Apparently, individuals who are unhappy at work are less likely to stay home from work when they cannot easily find alternative employment, perhaps due to concern about being fired for excessive absence.

Turnover

Most theories of turnover (people quitting their jobs) view it, at least in part, as the result of employee job dissatisfaction (Bartunek, Huang, & Walsh, 2008; Mobley, Griffeth, Hand, & Meglino, 1979; Wilke et al., 2018). People who dislike their jobs or a facet important to them will attempt to find alternative employment that they believe they will like better. Studies have been reasonably consistent in showing a correlation between job satisfaction and turnover intentions (Kim & Kao, 2014) and turnover itself (Rubenstein, Eberly, Lee, & Mitchell, 2018). One complication is that whether job dissatisfaction translates into turnover is affected by being able to find another job. This is supported by a meta-analysis that shows how unemployment rate at the time of a study moderates the job satisfaction-turnover relationship (Carsten & Spector, 1987). The correlation is strong when the unemployment rate is low and jobs are plentiful, and the correlation is weak when the unemployment rate is high, making it challenging to find another job.

Models of turnover place job satisfaction in the center of a complex process that involves factors both inside and outside of the employing organization. Figure 6.2 is a model that illustrates this process. Characteristics of the individual combine with characteristics of the job environment in determining level of job satisfaction. If the job satisfaction level is sufficiently low, the person will develop a behavioral intention to quit the job. That intention may lead to job search activities, which if successful will lead to turnover. Alternate employment opportunities are important because a person is not likely to quit without another job offer.

Turnover is one outcome that we have confidence is due to job dissatisfaction. This is because the nature of the research design in turnover studies allows for the assessment of job satisfaction before the turnover event occurs. Thus we can rule out the possibility that turnover caused the report of job satisfaction (such design strategies are discussed in Spector, 2019). In the typical turnover study, job satisfaction is measured in a sample of employees at one point in time. Months or even a year later, the researcher determines who has quit to see if job satisfaction can predict turnover. It is clear with this design that the direction of effects must run from job satisfaction to turnover rather than the reverse because the behavior did not occur until well after the job satisfaction assessment. Of course, it is possible that job satisfaction itself was not the causal factor but was associated with the causal factor—the determination of causality is never certain.

There is good research support for the connections among the variables in Figure 6.2. The antecedents of job satisfaction itself were discussed in Chapters 4 and 5. Both employee and workplace factors have been found to jointly result in job satisfaction. Job satisfaction correlates quite well with

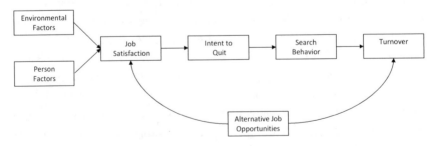

Figure 6.2 Model of employee turnover as a function of job satisfaction and the unemployment rate.

intention of quitting the job and turnover (Rubenstein et al., 2018; Tett & Meyer, 1993). Furthermore, Blau (1993) found that intention to quit related to job search behaviors ($r = 0.27, 0.25$ in two samples). Search behaviors include:

- Contacting an employment agency.
- Preparing or revised a resumé.
- Sending resumés to employers.
- Going on job interviews.

Blau showed that these behaviors were the strongest predictor of subsequent turnover with a correlation of 0.43 and 0.41 in two samples. By contrast the correlations in his samples between job satisfaction and turnover were only -0.16 and -0.15, which are not far from the mean of -0.25 found by Tett and Meyer (1993) in their meta-analysis.

So far turnover has been approached as a reaction by individuals to the work environment. Judge (1993) hypothesized that the affective disposition (NA) of the individual would interact with job satisfaction in influencing decisions to quit the job. Based on the work of Weitz (1952), he hypothesized that people low on NA had a general tendency to be satisfied in life, would have a more difficult time handling a dissatisfying job, and would be more likely to quit when they were unhappy at work. Those high on NA would be more used to being in a dissatisfied and negative emotional state, and so they would have less of a reaction to a dissatisfying job. Consistent with predictions, affective disposition moderated the job satisfaction-turnover relationship. For those low in NA, there was a large difference in turnover rates between those who were satisfied (6%) and dissatisfied (32%). For those high in NA, the turnover rates were not very different (10% versus 15%). The results of this study underscore how characteristics of the employee interact with characteristics of the organization in determining behavior.

References

Andel, S. A., Kessler, S. R., Pindek, S., Kleinman, G., & Spector, P. E. (2019). Is cyberloafing more complex than we originally thought? Cyberloafing as a coping response to workplace aggression exposure. *Computers in Human Behavior, 101,* 124–130. doi: 10.1016/j.chb.2019.07.013

Bartunek, J. M., Huang, Z., & Walsh, I. J. (2008). The development of a process model of collective turnover. *Human Relations, 61,* 5–38. doi: 10.1177/0018726707085944

Benitez, M., & Medina, F. J. (2021). A work-unit level analysis of employees' well-being and service performance in hospitality industry. *Current Psychology: A Journal for Diverse Perspectives on Diverse Psychological Issues.* doi: 10.1007/s12144-021-01707-6

Berry, C. M., Carpenter, N. C., & Barratt, C. L. (2012). Do other-reports of counterproductive work behavior provide an incremental contribution over self-reports? A meta-analytic comparison. *Journal of Applied Psychology, 97,* 613–636. doi: 10.1037/a0026739

Blau, G. (1993). Further exploring the relationship between job search and voluntary individual turnover. *Personnel Psychology, 46,* 313–330. doi: 10.1111/j.1744-6570.1993.tb00876.x

Blau, G., Yang, Y., & Ward-Cook, K. (2006). Testing a measure of cyberloafing. *Journal of Allied Health, 35,* 9–17.

Bowling, N. A., & Beehr, T. A. (2006). Workplace harassment from the victim's perspective: A theoretical model and meta-analysis. *Journal of Applied Psychology, 91,* 998–1012. doi: 10.1037/0021-9010.91.5.998

Bowling, N. A., & Hammond, G. D. (2008). A meta-analytic examination of the construct validity of the Michigan Organizational Assessment Questionnaire Job Satisfaction Subscale. *Journal of Vocational Behavior, 73,* 63–77. doi: 10.1016/j.jvb.2008.01.004

Bowling, N. A., Khazon, S., Meyer, R. D., & Burrus, C. J. (2015). Situational strength as a moderator of the relationship between job satisfaction and job performance: A meta-analytic examination. *Journal of Business and Psychology, 30,* 89–104. doi: 10.1007/s10869-013-9340-7

Brown, S. P., & Lam, S. K. (2008). A meta-analysis of relationships linking employee satisfaction to customer responses. *Journal of Retailing, 84,* 243–255. doi: 10.1016/j.jretai.2008.06.001

Caldwell, D. F., & O'Reilly, C. A. (1990). Measuring person-job fit with a profile-comparison process. *Journal of Applied Psychology, 75,* 648–657. doi: 10.1037/0021-9010.75.6.648

Carpenter, N. C., Berry, C. M., & Houston, L. (2014). A meta-analytic comparison of self-reported and other-reported organizational citizenship behavior. *Journal of Organizational Behavior, 35,* 547–574. doi: 10.1002/job.1909

Carsten, J. M., & Spector, P. E. (1987). Unemployment, job satisfaction, and employee turnover: A meta-analytic test of the Muchinsky model. *Journal of Applied Psychology, 72,* 374–381. doi: 10.1037/0021-9010.72.3.374

Cook, A. W. (2017). *Cyberloafing, job satisfaction, and employee productivity: A quantitative study.* D.B.A., ProQuest Dissertations & Theses A&I; ProQuest Dissertations & Theses Global database. (10615774), Ann Arbor, MI: Northcentral University.

Dalal, R. S. (2005). A meta-analysis of the relationship between organizational citizenship behavior and counterproductive work behavior. *Journal of Applied Psychology, 90,* 1241–1255. doi: 10.1037/0021-9010.90.6.1241

Dalton, D. R., & Mesch, D. J. (1991). On the extent and reduction of avoidable absenteeism: An assessment of absence policy provisions. *Journal of Applied Psychology, 76,* 810–817. doi: 10.1037/0021-9010.76.6.810

Farrell, D., & Stamm, C. L. (1988). Meta-analysis of the correlates of employee absence. *Human Relations, 41,* 211–227. doi: 10.1177/001872678804100302

Fox, S., Spector, P. E., Goh, A., Bruursema, K., & Kessler, S. R. (2012). The deviant citizen: Measuring potential positive relations between counterproductive work behaviour and organizational citizenship behaviour. *Journal of Occupational and Organizational Psychology, 85,* 199–220. doi: 10.1111/j.2044-8325.2011.02032.x

Franke, G. R., & Park, J.-E. (2006). Salesperson Adaptive Selling Behavior and Customer Orientation: A Meta-Analysis. *Journal of Marketing Research, 43,* 693–702. doi: 10.1509/jmkr.43.4.693

Goff, S. J. M., Michael K., & Jamison, R. L. (1990). Employer supported child care, work/family conflict, and absenteeism: A field study. *Personnel Psychology, 43,* 793–809. doi: 10.1111/j.1744-6570.1990.tb00683.x

Haccoun, R. R., & tale Jeanrie, C. (1995). Self reports of work absence as a function of personal attitudes towards absence, and perceptions of the organisation. *Applied Psychology, 44,* 155–170. doi: 10.1111/j.1464-0597.1995.tb01072.x

Hammer, T. H., & Landau, J. (1981). Methodological issues in the use of absence data. *Journal of Applied Psychology, 66,* 574–581. doi: 10.1037/0021-9010.66.5.574

Harter, J. K., Schmidt, F. L., & Hayes, T. L. (2002). Business-unit-level relationship between employee satisfaction, employee engagement, and business outcomes: A meta-analysis. *Journal of Applied Psychology, 87,* 268–279. doi: 10.1037/0021-9010.87.2.268

Henle, C. A., & Blanchard, A. L. (2008). The interaction of work stressors and organizational sanctions on cyberloafing. *Journal of Managerial Issues, 20*, 383–400.

Hershcovis, M. S., Turner, N., Barling, J., Arnold, K. A., Dupre, K. E., Inness, M., LeBlanc, M. M., & Sivanathan, N. (2007). Predicting workplace aggression: A meta-analysis. *Journal of Applied Psychology, 92*, 228–238. doi: 10.1037/0021-9010.92.1.228

Jacobs, R., & Solomon, T. (1977). Strategies for enhancing the prediction of job performance from job satisfaction. *Journal of Applied Psychology, 62*, 417–421. doi: 10.1037/0021-9010.62.4.417

Judge, T. A. (1993). Does affective disposition moderate the relationship between job satisfaction and voluntary turnover? *Journal of Applied Psychology, 78*, 395–401.

Judge, T. A., Thoresen, C. J., Bono, J. E., & Patton, G. K. (2001). The job satisfaction–job performance relationship: A qualitative and quantitative review. *Psychological Bulletin, 127*, 376–407. doi: 10.1037/0033-2909.127.3.376

Kessler, S. R., Lucianetti, L., Pindek, S., Zhu, Z., & Spector, P. E. (2020). Job satisfaction and firm performance: Can employees' job satisfaction change the trajectory of a firm's performance? *Journal of Applied Social Psychology, 50*, 563–572. doi: 10.1111/jasp.12695

Kim, H., & Kao, D. (2014). A meta-analysis of turnover intention predictors among US child welfare workers. *Children and Youth Services Review, 47*, 214–223. doi: 10.1016/j.childyouth.2014.09.015

Kohler, S. S., & Mathieu, J. E. (1993). Individual characteristics, work perceptions, and affective reactions influences on differentiated absence criteria. *Journal of Organizational Behavior, 14*, 515–530. doi: 10.1002/job.4030140602

Koys, D. J. (2001). The effects of employee satisfaction, organizational citizenship behavior and turnover on organizational effectiveness: A unit-level longitudinal study. *Personnel Psychology, 54*, 101–114. doi: 10.1111/j.1744-6570.2001.tb00087.x

Lim, V. K. G. (2002). The IT way of loafing on the job: cyberloafing, neutralizing and organizational justice. *Journal of Organizational Behavior, 23*, 675–694. doi: 10.1002/job.161

Martocchio, J. J. (1994). The effects of absence culture on individual absence. *Human Relations, 47*, 243–262. doi: 10.1177/001872679404700301

Mathieu, J. E., & Kohler, S. S. (1990). A cross-level examination of group absence influences on individual absence. *Journal of Applied Psychology, 75,* 217–220. doi: 10.1037/0021-9010.75.2.217

Mayfield, M., Mayfield, J., & Ma, K. Q. (2020). Innovation matters: creative environment, absenteeism, and job satisfaction. *Journal of Organizational Change Management, 33,* 715–735.

Mercado, B. K., Giordano, C., & Dilchert, S. (2017). A meta-analytic investigation of cyberloafing. *Career Development International, 22,* 546–564. doi: 10.1108/CDI-08-2017-0142

Mitra, A., Jenkins, G., & Gupta, N. (1992). A meta-analytic review of the relationship between absence and turnover. *Journal of Applied Psychology, 77,* 879–889. doi: 10.1037/0021-9010.77.6.879

Mobley, W. H., Griffeth, R. W., Hand, H. H., & Meglino, B. M. (1979). Review and conceptual analysis of the employee turnover process. *Psychological Bulletin, 86,* 493–522. doi: 10.1037/0033-2909.86.3.493

Nicholson, N., & Johns, G. (1985). The absence culture and the psychological contract: Who's in control of absence? *The Academy of Management Review, 10,* 397–407. doi: 10.2307/258123

Organ, D. W. (1997). Organizational citizenship behavior: It's construct clean-up time. *Human Performance, 10,* 85–97.

Organ, D. W., & Ryan, K. (1995). A meta-analytic review of attitudinal and dispositional predictors of organizational citizenship behavior. *Personnel Psychology, 48,* 775–802. doi: 10.1111/j.1744-6570.1995.tb01781.x

Öztürk, Y. E., Dömbekci, H. A., & Yesildal, M. (2018). The relationship between cyber loafing and job satisfaction in healthcare employee. *Journal of International Health Sciences and Management, 4,* 1–8.

Pindek, S., Krajcevska, A., & Spector, P. E. (2018). Cyberloafing as a coping mechanism: Dealing with workplace boredom. *Computers in Human Behavior, 86,* 147–152. doi: 10.1016/j.chb.2018.04.040

Pindek, S., & Spector, P. E. (2016). Organizational constraints: a meta-analysis of a major stressor. *Work & Stress, 30,* 7–25. doi: 10.1080/02678373.2015.1137376

Rubenstein, A. L., Eberly, M. B., Lee, T. W., & Mitchell, T. R. (2018). Surveying the forest: A meta-analysis, moderator investigation, and future-oriented discussion of the antecedents of voluntary employee turnover. *Personnel Psychology, 71,* 23–65. doi: 10.1111/peps.12226

Schaumberg, R. L., & Flynn, F. J. (2017). Clarifying the link between job satisfaction and absenteeism: The role of guilt proneness. *Journal of Applied Psychology, 102*, 982–992. doi: 10.1037/apl0000208.supp (Supplemental)

Schneider, B., Hanges, P. J., Smith, D. B., & Salvaggio, A. N. (2003). Which comes first: Employee attitudes or organizational financial and market performance? *Journal of Applied Psychology, 88*, 836–851. doi: 10.1037/0021-9010.88.5.836

Spector, P. E. (1997). The role of frustration in antisocial behavior at work. In R. A. Giacalone & J. Greenberg (Eds.), *Antisocial behavior in organizations* (pp. 1–17). Thousand Oaks, CA: Sage Publications, Inc.

Spector, P. E. (2019). Do not cross me: Optimizing the use of cross-sectional designs. *Journal of Business and Psychology, 34*, 125–137. doi: 10.1007/s10869-018-09613-8

Spector, P. E., Bauer, J. A., & Fox, S. (2010). Measurement artifacts in the assessment of counterproductive work behavior and organizational citizenship behavior: Do we know what we think we know? *Journal of Applied Psychology, 95*, 781–790. doi: 10.1037/a0019477

Spector, P. E., & Che, X. X. (2014). Re-examining citizenship: How the control of measurement artifacts affects observed relationships of organizational citizenship behavior and organizational variables. *Human Performance, 27*, 165–182. doi: 10.1080/08959285.2014.882928

Spector, P. E., & Fox, S. (2005). A model of counterproductive work behavior. In S. Fox & P. E. Spector (Eds.), *Counterproductive workplace behavior: Investigations of actors and targets* (pp. 151–174). Washington, DC: APA.

Storms, P. L., & Spector, P. E. (1987). Relationships of organizational frustration with reported behavioural reactions: The moderating effect of locus of control. *Journal of Occupational Psychology, 60*, 227–234. doi: 10.1111/j.2044-8325.1987.tb00255.x

Taris, T., & Schreurs, P. G. (2009). Well-being and organizational performance: An organizational-level test of the happy-productive worker hypothesis. *Work & Stress, 23*, 120–136. doi: 10.1080/02678370903072555

Tett, R. P., & Meyer, J. P. (1993). Job satisfaction, organizational commitment, turnover intention, and turnover: Path analyses base on meta-analytical findings. *Personnel Psychology, 46*, 259–293. doi: 10.1111/j.1744-6570.1993.tb00874.x

Vigoda-Gadot, E. (2006). Compulsory citizenship behavior: Theorizing some dark sides of the good soldier syndrome in organizations. *Journal for the Theory of Social Behaviour, 36*, 77–93. doi: 10.1111/j.1468-5914.2006.00297.x

Weissenfeld, K., Abramova, O., & Krasnova, H. (2019). *Antecedents for cyberloafing-a literature review.* Paper presented at the International Conference on Wirtschaftsinformatik, Siegen, Germany, February 24–27.

Weitz, J. (1952). A neglected concept in the study of job satisfaction. *Personnel Psychology, 5,* 201–205. doi: 10.1111/j.1744-6570.1952.tb01012.x

Wilke, D. J., Radey, M., King, E., Spinelli, C., Rakes, S., & Nolan, C. R. (2018). A multi-level conceptual model to examine child welfare worker turnover and retention decisions. *Journal of Public Child Welfare, 12,* 204–231. doi: 10.1080/15548732.2017.1373722

Zhang, Y., Crant, J. M., & Weng, Q. (2019). Role stressors and counterproductive work behavior: The role of negative affect and proactive personality. *International Journal of Selection and Assessment.* doi: 10.1111/ijsa.12255

7

PHYSICAL AND MENTAL HEALTH

An important question concerns whether working in a dissatisfying job has consequences for physical or mental health. Evidence shows that individuals who are in jobs that they dislike experience adverse physical and mental health outcomes (see meta-analysis by Faragher, Cass, & Cooper, 2013). These outcomes are often short-term physical health (e.g., digestive upset or headaches) and mental health (e.g., anxiety or depressed mood) symptoms. But what happens if people are stuck in dissatisfying jobs for an extended period? Might that contribute to more long-term or serious health issues? There are enough connections of job satisfaction with mental and physical health to raise concerns that jobs can be negatively affecting health.

Physical Health

Many studies have shown a link between physical health and job satisfaction. Researchers using self-report surveys have reported significant

DOI: 10.4324/9781003250616-7

correlations between job satisfaction and short-term physical or psychosomatic symptoms, such as headache and nausea (Peltokorpi & Ramaswami, 2021; Spector & Jex, 1998) that are associated with stress. Furthermore, Bruk-Lee, Nixon, and Spector (2013) found a negative correlation between job satisfaction and cardiovascular disease factors. Dissatisfied employees were more likely than their satisfied counterparts to report being diagnosed with coronary disease, elevated cholesterol or triglycerides, and hypertension. The reason for this connection is not entirely certain, but it is likely that job stress is the mechanism as it has been linked to cardiovascular disease (Steptoe & Kivimäki, 2013) as well as job dissatisfaction as I discussed in Chapter 4. Job stress is a likely contributor to other aspects of physical and mental health as I will note throughout this chapter.

Attempts to link job satisfaction to more direct momentary psychophysiological measures of health (e.g., blood pressure, cortisol levels, epinephrine, and heart rate) not dependent on employee self-reports have been less fruitful. For example, several studies have failed to find a connection between job satisfaction and employee blood pressure (Fox, Dwyer, & Ganster, 1993; Melamed, Ben-Avi, Luz, & Green, 1995; Wright, Cropanzano, Bonett, & Diamond, 2009). In part the failure to find the connection might be because job satisfaction is a relatively stable attitude, whereas blood pressure is something that fluctuates consistently over time due to many factors. Likely job satisfaction is not directly related to blood pressure and other psychophysiological measures, but rather some of the stressful aspects of work that might affect employee physiology could also lead to dissatisfaction.

Some hints about how people's job attitudes could influence their physiology come from job stress research done in Sweden (Johansson, 1981) with what are considered stress hormones. This line of research assessed catecholamine levels as people worked on machine-paced and self-paced jobs. The results showed that catecholamines associated with negative emotions increased when people did machine-paced jobs and decreased when they did self-paced jobs. The researchers speculated that performing jobs that caused distress (and presumably job dissatisfaction) led to increases in certain catecholamines.

There has been enough connection found between job satisfaction and physical health to produce concern. Even though much of the evidence is circumstantial, and measures of physical health are self-reported in most studies, it seems likely that job experiences are tied to health. Of course, the existence of an association does not mean than job dissatisfaction directly leads to poor health. It is possible that poor health can lead to dissatisfaction. However, job dissatisfaction is an important indicator of poor fit between and person and a job, and years spent in an unhappy work situation has the potential to contribute at least indirectly to poor health.

Accidents

A major threat to worker health is physical injury due to a workplace accident. There are many types of accidents including motor vehicle collisions, slipping on a wet floor, falling off a ladder or being injured with a tool or piece of equipment. There are also accidents that involve exposure to bio-hazardous (infectious disease) or toxic substances. Injuries due to accidents are prevalent in the workplace, with estimates as high as 100 million incidents annually worldwide (Barling & Frone, 2004).

Psychological factors play an important role in accidents, which occur as employees interact with their physical and social work environment. One such factor is job dissatisfaction. For example, Kim and Chung (2019) found that dissatisfaction was associated with traffic accidents in a sample of bus and taxi drivers. Probst, Jiang, and Graso (2016) found similar results with a sample of copper miners.

There are several possible explanations for the connection between dissatisfaction and accidents. One is that dissatisfied employees are less likely to follow organizational rules for safety, and it has been shown that dissatisfied employees are less likely to engage in safety behaviors (Cheng, Guo, & Lin, 2020). For example, Nixon et al. (2015) found that dissatisfaction among nurses was associated with their use of safety workarounds, that is, bypassing safety rules to get the job done. Another explanation is that the climate of an organization (see section on climate in Chapter 4) can lead to both accidents and satisfaction. An organization with a strong safety climate that shows concern of management for the welfare of workers is likely to have satisfied employees who follow safety rules that minimize accidents. Job satisfaction, safety climate, and accidents have been shown to all intercorrelate (Hutchinson, Andel, & Spector, 2018).

Musculoskeletal Disorder

Another aspect of workplace health is musculoskeletal disorder (MSD), which is pain in the bones, muscles, nerves, and tendons that can be due to over-exertion or repeated motions. The specific MSDs that people experience depends on the tasks they perform at work. MSDs can occur in the back from heavy lifting, neck from bending over a steering wheel, or wrists from typing. MSDs can occur in construction work that involves heavy tools and equipment, manufacturing where people perform the same motions repeatedly in assembling a product, or office work from too much time sitting in front of a computer screen.

Although MSDs are the byproduct of physical motions that produce inflammation or injury, there is a psychological component as well. Studies have shown that MSDs are clearly connected to stress on the job (Sobeih, Salem, Daraiseh, Genaidy, & Shell, 2006), and many of the stressors I discussed in Chapter 4 are related to experiencing MSDs. One clear psychological factor found to predict MSDs is job dissatisfaction (Stewart et al., 2014). For example, Dick, Lowe, Lu, and Krieg (2015) asked people if they liked their jobs and found that people who responded "no" were twice as likely to report having back pain. The connection between job dissatisfaction and MSDs is likely complex, but one mechanism suggested that dissatisfaction is an indicator that a job is stressful, and stress can lead to increased muscle tension that contributes to MSDs (Amiri & Behnezhad, 2020).

Violence

For some industries and occupations, such as healthcare or policing, physical violence can be a common occurrence. In a meta-analysis of 160 studies of nurses, Spector, Zhou, and Che (2014) found that more than a third had experienced physical violence at least once at work, and a third had been injured in a workplace physical attack. As with accidents, there is a relationship between job satisfaction and physical violence, with dissatisfied employees being more likely to be assaulted at work (Kessler, Spector, Chang, & Parr, 2008). Further, some of the same mechanisms might be at play in the connection. First, a dissatisfied employee might behave in a way that makes assault more likely (e.g., a nurse is rude to a patient who is upset). Second, the climate of an organization might influence both job satisfaction of employees and the likelihood of assault. Third, it seems likely that physical violence is a stressor that leads to dissatisfaction, and most studies that connect job satisfaction with violence have approached it from that perspective (e.g., Yoon & Sok, 2016).

Mental Health

Job satisfaction can be considered a general indicator of work adjustment that can be relevant to mental health. In fact, high levels of job satisfaction can reflect positive mental health and well-being. But what happens to people who are dissatisfied with their jobs. Might their mental health be negatively affected?

There are three aspects of mental health that are typically studied in relation to job satisfaction.

- **Subclinical mental health symptoms**. These are negative emotions at work that everyone experiences from time to time, such as anxiety or depressed mood.
- **Diagnosed mental health disorders**. These include anxiety disorders, clinical depression, or substance abuse.
- **Positive mental health**. This is not just the absence of mental health symptoms or disorders, but is positive well-being that indicates a high level of emotional and social functioning.

Studies of mental health symptoms often assess distress and specific negative emotions, most notably anger, anxiety, and depressed mood. Other studies will use measures of general mental health. Job satisfaction has been shown to relate to both types of measures. Job dissatisfaction has been associated with high levels of negative emotions (e.g., Van Katwyk, Fox, Spector, & Kelloway, 2000; Yang, Liu, Nauta, Caughlin, & Spector, 2016), such as anxiety and depression (Pyc, Meltzer, & Liu, 2017). Job dissatisfaction has also been associated with low scores on general measures of mental health, although these do not necessarily reflect clinical disorders (Cass, Siu, Faragher, & Cooper, 2003). This line of research has established a link between job satisfaction and mental health, but as with physical health, it is not clear that dissatisfaction itself leads to poor mental health.

Rather it might be an indicator of problematic job conditions that adversely affect mental health. Of course, it is also possible that experiencing mental health symptoms and distress can lead to job dissatisfaction.

Burnout

Burnout is a distressed emotional/psychological state experienced on the job. Where job satisfaction is an attitudinal response, burnout is more of an emotional response to the job. Burnout theory proposes that a person who is in a state of burnout experiences symptoms of emotional exhaustion and low work motivation, not unlike depression. The work on burnout originally came from research on direct care employees, such as nurses or social workers. It was felt by early burnout researchers that providing direct care to people in need led to symptoms of burnout not likely to be experienced by employees in other types of work. In recent years, burnout research has been conducted with many types of jobs that do not involve direct care of people.

According to Maslach (1998), there are three components of burnout:

- **Depersonalization** is the emotional distancing from direct care clients that results in a callous and uncaring attitude toward others. It indicates a low level of engagement and motivation.
- **Emotional exhaustion** is the feeling of fatigue and lack of enthusiasm for work.
- **Reduced personal accomplishment** is the sense that nothing of value is being done at work by the person.

As might be expected, burnout correlates significantly with job satisfaction in that dissatisfied employees are likely to report high levels of burnout (Senol-Durak, Durak, & Gencoz, 2021; Skaalvik & Skaalvik, 2021; Yang & Caughlin, 2017). Lee and Ashforth (1993) found stronger relations between job satisfaction and emotional exhaustion ($r = -0.50$) than with depersonalization ($r = -0.33$) or personal accomplishment ($r = 0.28$). Note that personal accomplishment is scored so that low scores reflect high burnout, which is opposite to the other burnout subscales. Burnout also correlates significantly with many variables that are correlates of job satisfaction. For example, high burnout levels have been associated with low levels of control and life satisfaction, and high levels of health symptoms and intention of quitting the job (Cordes & Dougherty, 1993).

A model of burnout was developed by Lee and Ashforth (1993) which hypothesized a chain of events from job conditions to job satisfaction to burnout. They explained that emotional exhaustion is a reaction to the negative feelings a person has when in a dissatisfying job. The other components of burnout follow from emotional exhaustion. Using complex statistical procedures of structural equation modeling, Lee and Ashforth found support for their model.

Mental Health Disorders

As noted, job satisfaction is associated with subclinical mental health symptoms of emotional distress. An important question is whether job dissatisfaction is associated with mental health disorders themselves. A large-scale Danish study with more than 13,000 workers shows a link between being dissatisfied at work and having a diagnosed mental health disorder, specifically anxiety, depression, or substance abuse (Jensen, Wieclaw, Munch-Hansen, Thulstrup, & Bonde, 2010). Similarly, Brown et al. (2020) used self-report mental disorder screening instruments for anxiety, depression, and post-traumatic stress disorders among United Nations employees. Job dissatisfaction was associated with all three types of disorders.

These studies merely show that job satisfaction is associated with mental health disorders, but they do not establish that dissatisfaction itself can trigger them. More likely it is stressful job conditions that are the contributors to mental health disorders (LaMontagne, Keegel, Louie, & Ostry, 2010). People who experience excessive job stress might experience emotional distress that can reach the clinical level. Those same stressful conditions can also lead to job dissatisfaction.

Substance Abuse

As with mental health disorders, there is some evidence linking job dissatisfaction to alcohol and drug use (Martin & Roman, 1996). There is also some evidence that people who are dissatisfied with work are more likely to abuse alcohol and other drugs (Galaif, Newcomb, & Carmona, 2001). This does not mean that people necessarily turn to alcohol and drugs to cope with dissatisfying jobs. In their longitudinal study, Galaif et al. (2001) found evidence that job dissatisfaction was more likely the effect of substance abuse rather than the cause. Further, the connection between substance abuse and job satisfaction is more likely due to job stress (Frone, 1999), and in at least one study it was job stress and not job satisfaction that was related to substance abuse (Tomczyk, Pedersen, Hanewinkel, Isensee, & Morgenstern, 2016).

With both mental health disorders and substance abuse, job satisfaction itself is unlikely the cause. More likely it is a concomitant phenomenon that is associated with job conditions that are contributing to mental health issues. As such is can be a useful indicator because when satisfaction is low there are likely problems with the job that might be detrimental to mental and physical health of employees. This is another reason that monitoring and managing job satisfaction is important, as it serves as a warning signal that there are employee issues that need attention.

Life Satisfaction

The positive side of mental health is not just the absence of mental health symptoms or mental health disorders. It reflects a high level of positive well-being. In a sense, job satisfaction might be considered such an indicator as high levels suggest good adjustment to work, and positive feelings about one important domain of life. But overall positive well-being goes beyond work into all aspects of life. The interplay of work and nonwork is an important ingredient in understanding people's reactions to jobs. We tend to study work mainly in the workplace, but employees are influenced by events and situations outside of their place of work. Conversely, behavior and feelings about nonwork are influenced by experience on the job.

Life satisfaction refers to a person's feelings about life in general. It can be assessed on the facet level as satisfaction with specific areas of life, such as family or recreation. It can also be assessed globally, as overall satisfaction with life. Since life satisfaction reflects overall feelings about life, it is considered a measure of well-being, with high scores reflecting positive mental health.

Since work is a major component of life for people who are employed, it seems obvious that job satisfaction and life satisfaction should be related.

Three hypotheses have been discussed about how job and life satisfaction are linked (Rain, Lane, & Steiner, 1991).

- **The spillover hypothesis** suggests that feelings in one area of life affect feelings in other areas. A person who is satisfied on the job is likely to be satisfied with life in general. Thus, job and life satisfaction should be positively related.
- **The compensation hypothesis** states that people will compensate for dissatisfaction in one area of life by cultivating satisfaction in another. A person with a dissatisfying job will put the majority of his or her energy into nonwork activities, while someone with a dissatisfying nonwork life may put most of their effort into work. This leads to a negative relationship between job and life satisfaction.
- **The segmentation hypothesis** posits that people compartmentalize their lives, making work and nonwork separate. Job and life satisfaction, therefore, will be unrelated.

The research findings in this domain clearly favor the spillover hypothesis. Studies consistently find that job satisfaction and life satisfaction are moderately and positively correlated. For example, Gonzalez-Mulé, Carter, and Mount (2017) found a mean correlation between the two of 0.44 across 57 studies in their meta-analysis. Bowling, Eschleman, and Wang (2010) investigated relationships between job satisfaction facets and life satisfaction, finding significant mean correlations for coworkers, pay, promotion, supervision, and work itself. The correlation between job satisfaction and life satisfaction alone does not offer much insight into which might cause which. It is possible that job satisfaction causes life satisfaction, or the reverse. A longitudinal study by Judge and Watanabe (1993) using complex statistical procedures of structural equation modeling provided evidence that both directions of causality are likely. That is, each type of satisfaction affects the other.

References

Amiri, S., & Behnezhad, S. (2020). Is job strain a risk factor for musculoskeletal pain? A systematic review and meta-analysis of 21 longitudinal studies. *Public Health, 181,* 158–167. doi: 10.1016/j.puhe.2019.11.023

Barling, J., & Frone, M. R. (2004). Occupational injuries: Setting the stage. In J. Barling & M. R. Frone (Eds.), *The psychology of workplace safety* (pp. 3–12). Washington, DC: APA.

Bowling, N. A., Eschleman, K. J., & Wang, Q. (2010). A meta-analytic examination of the relationship between job satisfaction and subjective well-being. *Journal of Occupational and Organizational Psychology, 83,* 915–934. doi: 10.1348/096317909X478557

Brown, A. D., Schultebraucks, K., Qian, M., Li, M., Horesh, D., Siegel, C., Brody, Y., Amer, A. M., Lev-Ari, R. K., Mas, F., Marmar, C. R., & Farmer, J. (2020). Mental health disorders and utilization of mental healthcare services in United Nations personnel. *Global Mental Health, 7,* e5. doi: 10.1017/gmh.2019.29

Bruk-Lee, V., Nixon, A. E., & Spector, P. E. (2013). An expanded typology of conflict at work: Task, relationship and non-task organizational conflict as social stressors. *Work & Stress, 27,* 339–350. doi: 10.1080/02678373.2013.841303

Cass, M. H., Siu, O. L., Faragher, E., & Cooper, C. L. (2003). A meta-analysis of the relationship between job satisfaction and employee health in Hong Kong. *Stress and Health: Journal of the International Society for the Investigation of Stress, 19,* 79–95.

Cheng, L., Guo, H., & Lin, H. (2020). The influence of leadership behavior on miners' work safety behavior. *Safety Science, 132.* doi: 10.1016/j.ssci.2020.104986

Cordes, C. L., & Dougherty, T. W. (1993). A review and an integration of research on job burnout. *The Academy of Management Review, 18,* 621–656. doi: 10.2307/258593

Dick, R. B., Lowe, B. D., Lu, M.-L., & Krieg, E. F. (2015). Further trends in work-related musculoskeletal disorders: A comparison of risk factors for symptoms using quality of work life data from the 2002, 2006, and 2010 general social survey. *Journal of Occupational and Environmental Medicine, 57,* 910–928. doi: 10.1097/JOM.0000000000000501

Faragher, E. B., Cass, M., & Cooper, C. L. (2013). The relationship between job satisfaction and health: A meta-analysis. In C. L. Cooper (Ed.), *From stress to wellbeing volume 1: The theory and research on occupational stress and wellbeing* (pp. 254–271). London: Palgrave Macmillan UK.

Fox, M. L., Dwyer, D. J., & Ganster, D. C. (1993). Effects of stressful job demands and control on physiological and attitudinal outcomes in a hospital setting. *Academy of Management Journal, 36,* 289–318. doi: 10.2307/256524

Frone, M. R. (1999). Work stress and alcohol use. *Alcohol Research & Health: The Journal of the National Institute on Alcohol Abuse and Alcoholism, 23,* 284–291.

Galaif, E. R., Newcomb, M. D., & Carmona, J. V. (2001). Prospective relationships between drug problems and work adjustment in a community sample of adults. *Journal of Applied Psychology, 86,* 337–350. doi: 10.1037/0021–9010.86.2.337

Gonzalez-Mulé, E., Carter, K. M., & Mount, M. K. (2017). Are smarter people happier? Meta-analyses of the relationships between general mental ability and job and life satisfaction. *Journal of Vocational Behavior, 99,* 146–164. doi: 10.1016/j.jvb.2017.01.003

Hutchinson, D. M., Andel, S. A., & Spector, P. E. (2018). Digging deeper into the shared variance among safety-related climates: the need for a general safety climate measure. *International Journal of Occupational and Environmental Health, 24,* 38–46. doi: 10.1080/10773525.2018.1507867

Jensen, H. K., Wieclaw, J., Munch-Hansen, T., Thulstrup, A. M., & Bonde, J. P. (2010). Does dissatisfaction with psychosocial work climate predict depressive, anxiety and substance abuse disorders? A prospective study of Danish public service employees. *Journal of Epidemiology and Community Health, 64,* 796–801. doi: 10.1136/jech.2008.083980

Johansson, G. (1981). Psychoneuroendocrine correlates of unpaced and paced performance. In G. Salvendy & M. J. Smith (Eds.), *Machine pacing and occupational stress* (pp. 277–286). London: Taylor & Francis.

Judge, T. A., & Watanabe, S. (1993). Another look at the job satisfaction-life satisfaction relationship. *Journal of Applied Psychology, 78,* 939–948. doi: 10.1037/0021-9010.78.6.939

Kessler, S. R., Spector, P. E., Chang, C.-H., & Parr, A. D. (2008). Organizational violence and aggression: Development of the three-factor Violence Climate Survey. *Work & Stress, 22,* 108–124. doi: 10.1080/0267837080218726

Kim, S. J., & Chung, E. K. (2019). The effect of organizational justice as perceived by occupational drivers on traffic accidents: Mediating effects of job satisfaction. *Journal of Safety Research, 68,* 27–32. doi: 10.1016/j.jsr.2018.11.001

LaMontagne, A. D., Keegel, T., Louie, A. M., & Ostry, A. (2010). Job stress as a preventable upstream determinant of common mental disorders: A review for practitioners and policy-makers. *Advances in Mental Health, 9,* 17–35. doi: 10.5172/jamh.9.1.17

Lee, R. T., & Ashforth, B. E. (1993). A further examination of managerial burnout: Toward an integrated model. *Journal of Organizational Behavior, 14*, 3–20. doi: 10.1002/job.4030140103

Martin, J. K., & Roman, P. M. (1996). Job satisfaction, job reward characteristics, and employees' problem drinking behaviors. *Work and Occupations, 23*, 4–25. doi: 10.1177/0730888496023001002

Maslach, C. (1998). A multidimensional theory of burnout. In C. L. Cooper (Ed.), *Theories of organizational stress* (pp. 68–85). Oxford: Oxford University Press.

Melamed, S., Ben-Avi, I., Luz, J., & Green, M. S. (1995). Objective and subjective work monotony: Effects on job satisfaction, psychological distress, and absenteeism in blue-collar workers. *Journal of Applied Psychology, 80*, 29–42. doi: 10.1037/0021-9010.80.1.29

Nixon, A. E., Lanz, J. J., Manapragada, A., Bruk-Lee, V., Schantz, A., & Rodriguez, J. F. (2015). Nurse safety: How is safety climate related to affect and attitude? *Work & Stress*, 1–19. doi: 10.1080/02678373.2015.1076536

Peltokorpi, V., & Ramaswami, A. (2021). Abusive supervision and subordinates' physical and mental health: the effects of job satisfaction and power distance orientation. *The International Journal of Human Resource Management, 32*, 893–919. doi: 10.1080/09585192.2018.1511617

Probst, T. M., Jiang, L., & Graso, M. (2016). Leader–member exchange: Moderating the health and safety outcomes of job insecurity. *Journal of Safety Research, 56*, 47–56. doi: 10.1016/j.jsr.2015.11.003

Pyc, L. S., Meltzer, D. P., & Liu, C. (2017). Ineffective leadership and employees' negative outcomes: The mediating effect of anxiety and depression. *International Journal of Stress Management, 24*, 196–215. doi: 10.1037/str0000030

Rain, J. S., Lane, I. M., & Steiner, D. D. (1991). A current look at the job satisfaction/ life satisfaction relationship: Review and future considerations. *Human Relations, 44*, 287–307. doi: 10.1177/001872679104400305

Senol-Durak, E., Durak, M., & Gencoz, T. (2021). Job satisfaction, and burnout as mediators of trait anger, work stress, positive and negative affect in a sample of Turkish correctional officers. *Journal of Forensic Psychiatry & Psychology*. doi: 10.1080/14789949.2021.1884738

Skaalvik, E. M., & Skaalvik, S. (2021). Teacher burnout: Relations between dimensions of burnout, perceived school context, job satisfaction and motivation for teaching. A longitudinal study. *Teachers and Teaching: Theory and Practice, 26*(7–8). doi: 10.1080/13540602.2021.1913404

Sobeih, T. M., Salem, O., Daraiseh, N., Genaidy, A., & Shell, R. (2006). Psychosocial factors and musculoskeletal disorders in the construction industry: A systematic review. *Theoretical Issues in Ergonomics Science, 7,* 329–344. doi: 10.1080/14639220500090760

Spector, P. E., & Jex, S. M. (1998). Development of four self-report measures of job stressors and strain: Interpersonal conflict at work scale, organizational constraints scale, quantitative workload inventory, and physical symptoms inventory. *Journal of Occupational Health Psychology, 3,* 356–367. doi: 10.1037/1076-8998.3.4.356

Spector, P. E., Zhou, Z. E., & Che, X. X. (2014). Nurse exposure to physical and nonphysical violence, bullying, and sexual harassment: A quantitative review. *International Journal of Nursing Studies, 51,* 72–84. doi: 10.1016/j. ijnurstu.2013.01.010

Steptoe, A., & Kivimäki, M. (2013). Stress and cardiovascular disease: An update on current knowledge. *Annual Review of Public Health, 34,* 337–354. doi: 10.1146/annurev-publhealth-031912–114452

Stewart, S. K., Rothmore, P. R., Doda, D. V. D., Hiller, J. E., Mahmood, M. A., & Pisaniello, D. L. (2014). Musculoskeletal pain and discomfort and associated worker and organizational factors: A cross-sectional study. *Work: Journal of Prevention, Assessment & Rehabilitation, 48,* 261–271.

Tomczyk, S., Pedersen, A., Hanewinkel, R., Isensee, B., & Morgenstern, M. (2016). Polysubstance use patterns and trajectories in vocational students – A latent transition analysis. *Addictive Behaviors, 58,* 136–141. doi: 10.1016/j.addbeh.2016.02.027

Van Katwyk, P. T., Fox, S., Spector, P. E., & Kelloway, E. (2000). Using the Job-Related Affective Well-Being Scale (JAWS) to investigate affective responses to work stressors. *Journal of Occupational Health Psychology, 5,* 219–230. doi: 10.1037/1076-8998.5.2.219

Wright, T. A., Cropanzano, R., Bonett, D. G., & Diamond, W. J. (2009). The role of employee psychological well-being in cardiovascular health: When the twain shall meet. *Journal of Organizational Behavior, 30,* 193–208. doi: 10.1002/job.592

Yang, L.-Q., & Caughlin, D. E. (2017). Aggression-preventive supervisor behavior: Implications for workplace climate and employee outcomes. *Journal of Occupational Health Psychology, 22,* 1–18. doi: 10.1037/a0040148

Yang, L. Q., Liu, C., Nauta, M. M., Caughlin, D. E., & Spector, P. E. (2016). Be mindful of what you impose on your colleagues: Implications of social burden for burdenees' well-being, attitudes and counterproductive work behaviour. *Stress and Health: Journal of the International Society for the Investigation of Stress, 32,* 70–83. doi: 10.1002/smi.2581

Yoon, H. S., & Sok, S. R. (2016). Experiences of violence, burnout and job satisfaction in Korean nurses in the emergency medical centre setting. *International Journal of Nursing Practice, 22,* 596–604. doi: 10.1111/ijn.12479

8

INTERVENTIONS TO IMPROVE JOB SATISFACTION

As I discussed in the opening chapter, there are two main justifications for paying attention to job satisfaction: The humanitarian (taking care of people is the ethical and moral thing to do) and the pragmatic (job satisfaction affects the bottom line). For these reasons, job satisfaction is important to understand, and it is important that those who run organizations do what they can to maximize it.

Job satisfaction is easily assessed with employee surveys. Administered online, an entire organization can be assessed in a matter of days. Many organizations benchmark employee satisfaction and other variables such as engagement. Areas of the organization where employees are dissatisfied can be identified for possible intervention. Facet scales can pinpoint specific areas of concern. Often organizations will include targeted questions to address issues of local concern, such as new initiatives or policies.

There are many things that organizations can do to enhance job satisfaction once it is determined that there are areas needing improvement. Often organizations begin with employee surveys to determine the target

DOI: 10.4324/9781003250616-8

of intervention. The survey itself becomes the first step of the intervention that is based on employee input. Other times interventions are driven by management decisions about how best to improve the work experiences of employees. Some interventions are designed to improve the work environment, perhaps by redesigning the work. Other interventions are focused on employees to enhance their capabilities to handle job demands. There are a variety of interventions that can be effective in making the workplace better for employees and enhancing their job satisfaction.

Intervention Types

There are many kinds of interventions that organizations can undertake. Some can easily be conducted in-house, but others are best implemented with the help of experts who might be existing employees or external consultants. This is particularly the case when interventions are based on survey results. It takes expertise to properly design, conduct, and interpret results from an employee survey, and to plan appropriate responses. Furthermore, it is best to conduct follow-up evaluations to be sure that intended results were achieved, and to react if unintended negative consequences arise.

Survey Feedback

A potentially useful technique that many organizations have implemented successfully to enhance job satisfaction is survey feedback (Burke, 2018). With this procedure, diagnostic activities from employee input are combined with targeted interventions designed specifically for the organization. The first step is to conduct a job satisfaction survey of employees. Often this begins with focus group or individual interviews of employees to identify major issues. A questionnaire survey is then conducted that is informed by the interviews. Such a survey might include some facets measures that can be used as general benchmarks plus individual questions to get at specific local issues. The data are analyzed and placed into a report that is circulated to the employees who were surveyed. A committee consisting of employees and managers can be created to come up with recommendations based on the survey results. Top management reviews the recommendations and creates an action plan to implement changes. Not every suggestion needs to be adopted, but there should be a clear response to the feedback and an action plan executed.

Survey feedback has been demonstrated to be effective in enhancing the job satisfaction of employees (Bowers, 1973; Neuman, Edwards, & Raju, 1989). Although the diagnosis of organizational problems though job satisfaction surveys can be beneficial, they can also cause considerable damage if done improperly. One should be careful about undertaking diagnostic activities without a commitment to make positive changes based on them. The job satisfaction survey itself can raise expectations that management is concerned about employees. Lack of positive action following a survey is extremely frustrating to those who took the time to share concerns about the organization (Burke, 2018), leading to a negative response by employees that can be detrimental to the organization. Unfulfilled expectations can result in additional problems, such as counterproductive work behavior and turnover. To paraphrase an old saying, "better to let your employees believe you don't care about them than to take no action on a survey and prove it". At the very least, there should be discussions throughout the organization about what can and cannot be done following a survey. Employees need to understand why dissatisfying situations must exist. Note that sometimes explanations can have positive effects when employees are given a good reason for something being the way it is. For example, Greenberg (1990) showed that employees would accept a pay cut when they were told it was necessary due to the company's financial problems.

On the other hand, a properly conducted job satisfaction survey, when followed by a reasonable response, is an activity that can have tremendous payoffs. When employees are offered the opportunity to participate in decisions that affect them, positive benefits can accrue to both organizations and people.

Sociotechnical Systems Theory

Survey feedback is not the only type of organizational intervention that can improve organizations. Pasmore, Francis, Haldeman, and Shani (1982) reviewed the outcomes of 134 studies in which one or more features based on sociotechnical systems theory (Trist & Bamforth, 1951) were applied in the work place. This theory suggests an approach to organizational design that jointly optimizes people and technology so that people can perform well without undue stress. The applications included:

- Autonomous work teams that are self-managed and responsible for completing entire tasks, such as assembling an automobile.
- Creation of committees that can make recommendations to management.
- Feedback on performance.
- Quality control by employees on their own tasks.
- Team members selecting their own members.

Pasmore et al. (1982) found that out of 54 studies in which job satisfaction was measured, 94% had positive effects from sociotechnical systems interventions. It is not always clear that the implemented changes were the cause of the attitude enhancement as Hawthorne effects cannot be ruled out in many of these sorts of studies. Further, such changes are not always permanent as we saw with the Griffin (1991) job redesign study discussed in Chapter 4. Nevertheless, these sorts of interventions can be helpful in improving the workplace.

High-Performance Work Practices

Another type of intervention is based on HR actions characterized as "High-Performance Work Practices" or "Best Practices". These practices, some of which overlap with the sociotechnical systems interventions mentioned earlier, are linked to employee job satisfaction (Kooij, Jansen, Dikkers, & De Lange, 2010). Those that had the biggest effect, in order from largest to smallest were:

- **Job enrichment**: People are given high-scope jobs with flexibility and variety rather than simple highly structured tasks.
- **Performance management**: Performance appraisals are based on objective results and rewards are based on performance.
- **Teamwork**: There is an emphasis on employees working in teams.
- **Internal promotion**: There are opportunities for advancement within the organization. Some organizations have clear career ladders that specify the experiences and skills required for promotion.

- **Rewards**: Rewards are allocated fairly.
- **Staffing**: People have the right knowledge and skill for the job.
- **Participation**: Employees' input is sought about decisions concerning their jobs.

Decent Work

A more global point of view about satisfying jobs is the concept of decent work, promoted by the United Nations agency, the International Labour Organization (ILO). Decent work is the idea that everyone should have an opportunity to have a job that enables them to live a good life, be productive, and be safe (International Labour Organization, 2021). There are five areas that characterize decent work (McIlveen et al., 2021):

- **Safe conditions**: Both physical and psychological safety.
- **Access to healthcare**: Whether from the employer or government.
- **Adequate compensation**: Salary and rewards.
- **Time and rest**: Enough time for rest and nonwork activities.
- **Values congruence**: Match of employee and company values.

McIlveen et al. (2021) surveyed a wide cross-section of employees in Australia, finding that all but time and rest were significantly related to job satisfaction.

Enhancing Employee Capabilities

Organizations spend considerable resources in the training and development of their employees. Some of those activities are concerned with enhancing knowledge and skill to perform job tasks. Others focus on providing employees with tools to better manage health and well-being. A common approach is to provide various forms of stress management training.

A series of studies has demonstrated how well-being interventions can enhance job satisfaction. These include interventions to teach mindfulness (Vonderlin, Biermann, Bohus, & Lyssenko, 2020), stress management (Kröll, Doebler, & Nüesch, 2017), and yoga (Vonderlin et al., 2020). These interventions have the additional benefit of providing employees the capability of better handling the stress of their jobs.

Another approach with the potential to raise job satisfaction is to provide trained coaches who can help employees with professional development. This is most often done with mid-level managers and executives but can be provided to nonmanagerial employees as well. Research on executive coaching has shown positive effects on performance and on career satisfaction (Bozer, Sarros, & Santora, 2013). Jeannotte, Hutchinson, and Kellerman (2021) tracked more than 300 employees for six or more months as they interacted with their coaches. They found that indicators of positive mental health improved including self-efficacy and life satisfaction. Although they did not assess job satisfaction itself, many of the indicators they included are linked to job satisfaction.

Concluding Thoughts

This book has provided an overview of the vast literature on job satisfaction, covering assessment, potential antecedents, possible consequences, and how organizations might intervene to improve it. By necessity topics have been covered briefly, and some topics could not be covered at all given the space available. The serious student of this topic should consider this book as the initial introduction to the vast job satisfaction literature.

Beyond the research literature and studies, job satisfaction is important in everyday life. Organizations have tremendous effects on the people who work in them. Some of those effects, as this book has shown, are reflected in how people feel about work. Negative feelings can lead to behaviors that are detrimental to organizations, and potentially to adverse physical and psychological health. It is certainly within everyone's best interest for our organizations to function efficiently and smoothly. Organizational practices that maximize job satisfaction will likely have employees who are more cooperative and willing to help the organization be successful. It is also important that people maintain good health and positive well-being. Organizations can do much to help in this area by doing things to enhance job satisfaction.

Job satisfaction is an attitudinal variable that can be a diagnostic indicator of how a person is doing in one of the major domains of life. Job dissatisfaction suggests that a problem exists either in the job or in the person. As discussed in Chapter 4, many organizational conditions can lead to poor job attitudes. Also as discussed, sometimes events and factors outside of work can have negative effects on job satisfaction. These can include personal problems and societal issues. Job satisfaction on the other hand can be indicative of good work adjustment and positive well-being.

Many organizations conduct periodic job satisfaction surveys of employees to diagnose problem areas that demand management attention. Areas of job dissatisfaction, either facets that are unusually low or places (e.g., departments) that are lower than others, demand further investigation. Interventions designed to enhance job satisfaction can be tried. No single approach can be recommended for all cases as the problems are often idiosyncratic to each organization.

Job satisfaction has been a central variable in the study of people at work. It is relevant to both employees and their employing organizations. Job satisfaction can and should be managed as part of efforts to take care of human resources. It reflects that people are being well treated and that they are a good fit to their jobs. It can be considered an important indicator that should be benchmarked and tracked with periodic surveys that are an important tool for managing people. The study and understanding of job satisfaction are important for academics who research it and practitioners who manage it.

References

Bowers, D. G. (1973). OD techniques and their results in 23 organizations: The Michigan ICL study. *Journal of Applied Behavioral Science, 9*, 21–43. doi: 10.1177/002188637300900103

Bozer, G., Sarros, J. C., & Santora, J. C. (2013). The role of coachee characteristics in executive coaching for effective sustainability. *Journal of Management Development, 32*, 277–294. doi: 10.1108/02621711311318319

Burke, W. W. (2018). The rise and fall of the growth of organization development: What now? *Consulting Psychology Journal: Practice and Research, 70*, 186–206. doi: 10.1037/cpb0000116

Greenberg, J. (1990). "Employee theft as a reaction to underpayment inequity: The hidden cost of pay cuts": Correction. [Erratum/Correction]. *Journal of Applied Psychology, 75*, 667. doi: 10.1037/0021-9010.75.6.667

Griffin, R. W. (1991). Effects of work redesign on employee perceptions, attitudes, and behaviors: A long-term investigation. *Academy of Management Journal, 34*, 425–435. doi: 10.2307/256449

International Labour Organization. (2021). Decent work and the 2030 agenda for sustainable development, from https://www.ilo.org/global/topics/sdg-2030/lang-en/index.htm

Jeannotte, A. M., Hutchinson, D. M., & Kellerman, G. R. (2021). Time to change for mental health and well-being via virtual professional coaching: Longitudinal observational study. *Journal of Medical Internet Research, 23*, e27774. doi: 10.2196/27774

Kooij, D. T. A. M., Jansen, P. G. W., Dikkers, J. S. E., & De Lange, A. H. (2010). The influence of age on the associations between HR practices and both affective commitment and job satisfaction: A meta-analysis. *Journal of Organizational Behavior, 31*, 1111–1136. doi: 10.1002/job.666

Kröll, C., Doebler, P., & Nüesch, S. (2017). Meta-analytic evidence of the effectiveness of stress management at work. *European Journal of Work and Organizational Psychology, 26*, 677–693. doi: 10.1080/1359432X.2017.1347157

McIlveen, P., Hoare, P. N., Perera, H. N., Kossen, C., Mason, L., Munday, S., Alchin, C., Creed, A., & McDonald, N. (2021). Decent work's association with job satisfaction, work engagement, and withdrawal intentions in Australian working adults. *Journal of Career Assessment, 29*, 18–35. doi: 10.1177/1069072720922959

Neuman, G. A., Edwards, J. E., & Raju, N. S. (1989). Organizational development interventions: A meta-analysis of their effects on satisfaction and other attitudes. *Personnel Psychology, 42*, 461–489. doi: 10.1111/j.1744-6570.1989.tb00665.x

Pasmore, W. A., Francis, C., Haldeman, J., & Shani, A. (1982). Sociotechnical systems: A North American reflection on empirical studies of the seventies. *Human Relations, 35*, 1179–1204. doi: 10.1177/001872678203501207

Trist, E. L., & Bamforth, K. W. (1951). Some social and psychological consequences of the longwall method of coal-getting: An examination of the psychological situation and defences of a work group in relation to the social structure and technological content of the work system. *Human Relations, 4*, 3–38. doi: 10.1177/001872675100400101

Vonderlin, R., Biermann, M., Bohus, M., & Lyssenko, L. (2020). Mindfulness-based programs in the workplace: A meta-analysis of randomized controlled trials. *Mindfulness, 11*, 1579–1598. doi: 10.1007/s12671-020-01328-3

APPENDIX

Table A.1 The Job Satisfaction Survey

JOB SATISFACTION SURVEY
Copyright Paul E. Spector 1994, All rights reserved.

PLEASE CIRCLE THE ONE NUMBER FOR EACH QUESTION THAT COMES CLOSEST TO REFLECTING YOUR OPINION ABOUT IT.	Disagree Very Much	Disagree Moderately	Disagree Slightly	Agree Slightly	Agree Moderately	Agree Very Much
1. I feel I am being paid a fair amount for the work I do.	1	2	3	4	5	6
2. There is really too little chance for promotion on my job.	1	2	3	4	5	6
3. My supervisor is quite competent in doing his/her job.	1	2	3	4	5	6
4. I am not satisfied with the benefits I receive.	1	2	3	4	5	6
5. When I do a good job, I receive the recognition for it that I should receive.	1	2	3	4	5	6
6. Many of our rules and procedures make doing a good job difficult.	1	2	3	4	5	6
7. I like the people I work with.	1	2	3	4	5	6

(Continued)

PLEASE CIRCLE THE ONE NUMBER FOR EACH QUESTION THAT COMES CLOSEST TO REFLECTING YOUR OPINION ABOUT IT.	Disagree Very Much	Disagree Moderately	Disagree Slightly	Agree Slightly	Agree Moderately	Agree Very Much
8	I sometimes feel my job is meaningless.	1	2	3	4	5	6
9	Communications seem good within this organization.	1	2	3	4	5	6
10	Raises are too few and far between.	1	2	3	4	5	6
11	Those who do well on the job stand a fair chance of being promoted.	1	2	3	4	5	6
12	My supervisor is unfair to me.	1	2	3	4	5	6
13	The benefits we receive are as good as most other organizations offer.	1	2	3	4	5	6
14	I do not feel that the work I do is appreciated.	1	2	3	4	5	6
15	My efforts to do a good job are seldom blocked by red tape.	1	2	3	4	5	6
16	I find I have to work harder at my job because of the incompetence of people I work with.	1	2	3	4	5	6
17	I like doing the things I do at work.	1	2	3	4	5	6
18	The goals of this organization are not clear to me.	1	2	3	4	5	6
19	I feel unappreciated by the organization when I think about what they pay me.	1	2	3	4	5	6
20	People get ahead as fast here as they do in other places.	1	2	3	4	5	6
21	My supervisor shows too little interest in the feelings of subordinates.	1	2	3	4	5	6
22	The benefit package we have is equitable.	1	2	3	4	5	6
23	There are few rewards for those who work here.	1	2	3	4	5	6
24	I have too much to do at work.	1	2	3	4	5	6
25	I enjoy my coworkers.	1	2	3	4	5	6
26	I often feel that I do not know what is going on with the organization.	1	2	3	4	5	6
27	I feel a sense of pride in doing my job.	1	2	3	4	5	6
28	I feel satisfied with my chances for salary increases.	1	2	3	4	5	6
29	There are benefits we do not have which we should have.	1	2	3	4	5	6
30	I like my supervisor.	1	2	3	4	5	6
31	I have too much paperwork.	1	2	3	4	5	6
32	I don't feel my efforts are rewarded the way they should be.	1	2	3	4	5	6
33	I am satisfied with my chances for promotion.	1	2	3	4	5	6

34	There is too much bickering and fighting at work.	1	2	3	4	5	6
35	My job is enjoyable.	1	2	3	4	5	6
36	Work assignments are not fully explained.	1	2	3	4	5	6

Table A.2 Links to Resources from the Author's Website

Home Page for PaulSpector.com:
https://paulspector.com/

Assessment Archive:
https://paulspector.com/assessments/assessment-archive/

Job Satisfaction Survey, JSS:
https://paulspector.com/assessments/pauls-no-cost-assessments/
job-satisfaction-survey-jss/

Job Satisfaction Survey-2, JSS-2:
This is an improved commercial version of the JSS.
https://paulspector.com/assessments/job-satisfaction-survey-2/

Job Attitude Measures:
Instruments to measure attitude variables from the book.
https://paulspector.com/assessments/assessment-archive/
job-attitudes/

(Continued)

Paul's Page for the Book:
Videos and other content about job satisfaction.
https://paulspector.com/books/job-satisfaction/

Paul's Blog:
https://paulspector.com/blog/

About the Author:
https://paulspector.com/about-paul/

Note: I maintain a website that contains an assessment archive with links to the job satisfaction instruments in the book and other assessments used in job satisfaction research. I included some additional resources about job satisfaction on my page for the book. The website also hosts my weekly blog that deals with job satisfaction and related issues. This table contains links to the home page and other features likely of interest to readers of this book. Point your smart phone camera to the QR codes for quick access to these pages.

INDEX

Printed in the United States
by Baker & Taylor Publisher Services